T0151538

MINIATURE
JAPANESE GARDENS

BEAUTIFUL BONSAI LANDSCAPE
GARDENS FOR YOUR HOME

KENJI KOBAYASHI

TUTTLE Publishing

Tokyo | Rutland, Vermont | Singapore

Contents

Author's Note

Whether you live in the city or in the countryside, greenery nourishes the spirit. Being spiritually rich means having compassion for others and for the world as a whole. This kind of feeling is undeniably important. I believe that in order to have compassion for the different kinds of people in this world, it's important to be fully open and aware. Plants help us to become that way.

As we have been given four beautiful seasons, instead of just plodding from one busy day to the next, we should take time to appreciate deep emotion such as that which comes when a single flower blossoms on a cherry tree you raised yourself. It might only be for two weeks out of 365 days, but it's such a worthwhile experience, and to get there, one should think of caring for the tree not as a chore, but as something that brings joy. The tree gratefully takes in the water you give it and puts forth buds. Taking pleasure in caring for it elicits an awareness that can't be expressed in words. Awareness is vital because being tuned in to others' feelings—being aware of others besides ourselves—allows both self and others to be rescued. That's the kind of thing that plants teach us.

It's said that a bonsai tree is like a microcosm formed from the tree's inherent narrative or derived from its shape and form. Bonsai landscapes—recreating scenery in a pot—evoke pleasant associations and thoughts—"a tree I'd like to read beneath," or "let's spread a picnic blanket out under this tree and drink beer on a day off."

When starting out with bonsai landscapes, you may tend to think that raising these plants is difficult or labor-intensive, but it's far easier than raising pets or children. I hope this book will show you the fun of raising plants and enrich your spirit.

Kenji Kobayashi

PART ONE

Designing a Miniature Bonsai Landscape

Bonsai landscaping is a method by which scenery can be rendered in a pot according to one's own tastes. However, even if you have some experience with bonsai, making landscapes calls for a different approach. This section covers approaches to establishing various landscapes in pots—the number and composition of plants required to recreate such scenery and techniques for effective use of stones, ornamental sand and the like, comparing photos of landscapes and completed bonsai to illustrate and inspire.

Basic Bonsai Landscape Techniques

First of all, here are the instructions for creating the most basic of bonsai landscapes composed of a single seedling, moss and ornamental sand. Regardless of the type of bonsai landscape you're making, this is the basic method, so make sure to master it. Here, we will make a bonsai landscape with a single tree using a Chinese elm (*Ulmus parvifolia Jacq.*) and *Leucobryum juniperoideum*.

MATERIALS

Seedling

Chinese elm

Moss

Leucobryum juniperoideum

Soil

Compost

Stones to line pot

Fuji sand (large grain)

Ornamental sand

Maifan stones

METHOD

1. Place a net over the hole in the base of the pot and secure it with aluminum wire, then use the scoop to pour in stones to line the base (large grain Fuji sand). [see tools and instructions in part 5].

2. Use the scoop to add compost until the base stones are concealed.

3. Use pruning scissors to trim off old or damaged leaves. Check that there are no insects on the backs of the leaves.

4. Use the tips of your tweezers to brush off the soil around the roots a little at a time.

5. Draw out the roots and use scissors to trim the ends, adjusting the size of the upper section.

6. Hold the seedling in the pot and use a scoop to pour soil in.

7. Use a chopstick to work the soil into gaps around the roots, packing it in firmly.

8. Press the soil with a small spatula to release any air inside and make the soil more compact.

9. Spray the soil 3–5 times with an atomizer to firm it, making sure the water is absorbed.

10. Place a large piece of moss on the desired spot.

11. Using a chopstick at the edge of the moss to hold it in place, press the moss firmly into the soil.

12. Work in the same way to add more moss, taking care to make it look as if it's spreading naturally.

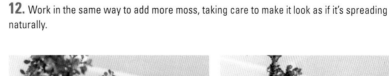

13. Use a scoop to add in ornamental gravel (Maifan stones) over areas where the soil is visible.

14. Use a spatula to level the ornamental gravel and make it neater

15. Complete by spraying it all over with an atomizer.

CHAPTER 1

Mountain Landscapes

MOUNTAIN LANDSCAPES ❶

A Forest Landscape with Moss

SCENERY FOR INSPIRATION

Serissa japonica and *Pleurozium schreberi* have been used to evoke the forests of Yakushima island, where humidity is high and everything is covered in a thick layer of moss. When you set foot in the forest to see its unusual plants and creatures, the mysterious atmosphere inspires a feeling of awe, which this work expresses.

COMPOSITION

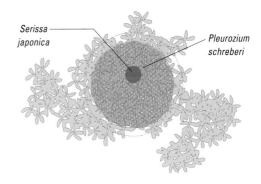

Plant *Serissa japonica* at the center and spread *Pleurozium schreberi* around it. *Pleurozium schreberi* is characterized by its tendency to spread up and along tree branches, and by incorporating it here the tree's surface will be covered, creating a pleasing texture. However, if it spreads too much over the pot it looks unkempt, so keep it within certain limits. To evoke an untouched wilderness, keep maintenance of the tree to a minimum by trimming off intersecting branches and the like, training the tree so it spreads outwards to achieve a horizontal form.

MOUNTAIN LANDSCAPES ❷

A Moss-Covered Wilderness

SCENERY FOR INSPIRATION

A bonsai of Chinese elm (*Ulmus parvifolia*) and *Pleurozium schreberi* calls to mind the forest landscape of Yaeyama, where a blanket of moss covers the trunks of huge trees. It's a vision of a paradise where plants grow luxuriantly and humidity cloaks the skin as soon as one steps into the forest.

COMPOSITION

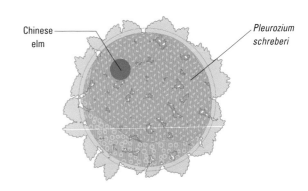

Working on a 7:3 ratio in the pot, plant the Chinese elm with its roots exposed, using soil to create a mound and covering it with *Pleurozium schreberi*. After three years, the moss has grown to cover the trunk, resulting in a characteristic texture. The leaves of the tree are dense and prone to mold, so be diligent in removing brown, withered leaves as part of its maintenance.

Tropical Jungle Scenery

SCENERY FOR INSPIRATION

A type of huge fern, *Angiopteris lygodiifolia*, stands in for a tropical rainforest lush with ferns, orchids and so on. The relaxed spreading leaves evoke the laid-back atmosphere of the tropics.

COMPOSITION

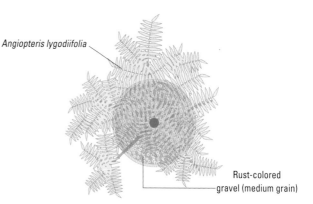

Angiopteris lygodiifolia is a low growing plant. Plant it in the center of the pot; after three years the leaves will form a pleasing shape. Place in dappled sunlight or partial shade and ensure it doesn't dry out. If fertilized properly, it will fill out nicely. It is hardy, so it makes a good decorative plant too.

A Plant Budding Secretly in the Mountains

SCENERY FOR INSPIRATION

Pictured here is a place deep in the mountains where not a soul treads and a plant reaches towards the sun after having grown quietly over time from a seed dropped in the soil by a bird. It's an expression of plants' courage and determination in nature's harsh struggle for existence.

COMPOSITION

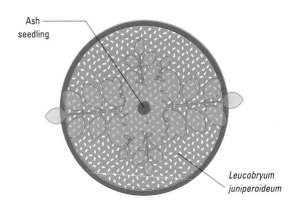

Ash seedling

Leucobryum juniperoideum

An ash (*Fraxinus japonica*) seedling is used because of the charm of its buds. Planted in the very center of the pot, its base is covered completely with *Leucobryum juniperoideum* to create a roundness of form. Ash trees are sturdy, and they serve to purify the air.

MOUNTAIN LANDSCAPES ❺

A Large, Ancient Tree

SCENERY FOR INSPIRATION

More than a century in age, the vitality and godliness of this tree convey its endurance of merciless natural forces, and the life force with which it continues to survive. In this work, that life force is expressed by way of the Chinese juniper (*Juniperus chinensis*) with a trunk that has been stripped and transformed into deadwood using the "shari" technique.

COMPOSITION

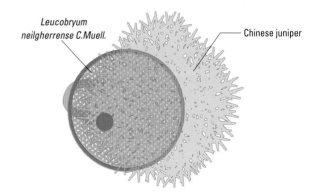

Leucobryum neilgherrense C.Muell.

Chinese juniper

Using the shari technique on the trunk of the Chinese juniper expresses the harshness of nature and creates a deeply rustic effect. Prune the tree so that the twisted trunk is shown to best effect, nipping off unwanted growth by hand. Plant in the pot working to a 7:3 ratio, covering the soil all around the tree with *Leucobryum neilgherrense C Muell.*

A North American River Landscape

SCENERY FOR INSPIRATION

Image © Sozaiya Hoshino

The majestic scenery of the US state of Oregon, with its backdrop of the Rocky Mountain range, formed the inspiration for this work. To express the dynamism of the landscape, Japanese cypresses (*Chamaecyparis obtusa*) are planted in a group, forming a forest of needle-leaved trees. Moss is used to create delicate undulations, while Ibigawa stones are placed to recall the tempestuous cliffs through which huge rivers run.

COMPOSITION

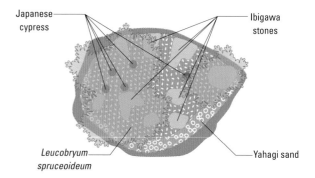

Japanese cypress — Ibigawa stones

Leucobryum spruceoideum — Yahagi sand

First of all, create a large mountain on a shallow stone plate. Group several Japanese cypress together (five were used in this work), with one large tree, two small ones and two of a size in-between to create differences in height. If there is a tree lacking in branches, plant others in front, to the left, right and back of it to compensate and achieve the appearance of a forest. Planting trees from the mountain summit towards the back of the arrangement gives the impression that the forest continues.

A Pristine Rushing Waterfall

SCENERY FOR INSPIRATION

This piece draws on the cool sensation of a waterfall flowing with pure, clear water and forming a backdrop to a tranquil spot deep in the mountains where plants of all kinds thrive. The Japanese maple (*Acer amoenum*) and Japanese forest grass (*Hakonechloa macra*) express the refreshingly cool breeze blowing through the gaps between the waterfall and the trees.

COMPOSITION

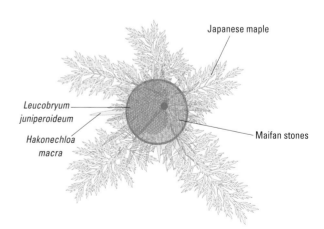

Japanese maple

Leucobryum juniperoideum

Hakonechloa macra

Maifan stones

Position the Japanese maple in the pot working to a 7:3 ratio. When planting, make sure the branches trail towards the pot in order to achieve a feeling of stability. Hide the base with Japanese forest grass. Creating different heights in the work via the grass and the tree lends the piece a natural feel.

15

A Lone Tree in a Grassy Field

SCENERY FOR INSPIRATION

This work calls to mind the image of a single large tree growing in a grassy open space bathed in brilliant sunlight. It evokes the kind of tranquil scenery in which, on a clear spring day, the passing of time is forgotten and the day is given over to leisure in the shade of a tree.

COMPOSITION

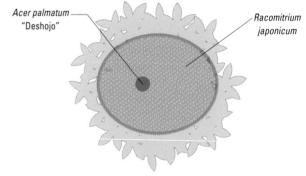

Acer palmatum "Deshojo"

Racomitrium japonicum

With its thick trunk and air of a large tree, this Japanese maple (*Acer palmatum* "Deshojo") should be positioned in the pot working to a 7:3 ratio with the moss spread around it. Spread the branches out horizontally on all sides in order to make the tree appear even larger in the pot, but decide on a perimeter and prune the branches so they do not extend beyond it. I used a shallow flat pot to showcase the work's stability and the spreading branches.

A Small Tree on a Vast Hillside

SCENERY FOR INSPIRATION

This work calls to mind the image of a single large tree growing in a grassy open space bathed in brilliant sunlight. It evokes the kind of tranquil scenery in which, on a clear spring day, the passing of time is forgotten and the day is given over to leisure in the shade of a tree.

COMPOSITION

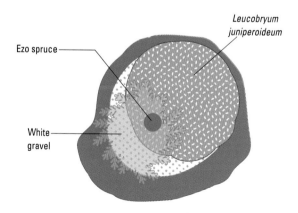

Ezo spruce

Leucobryum juniperoideum

White gravel

Use clay soil on a shallow stone plate to build the framework for the piece, then add compost. Plant the Ezo spruce (*Picea jezoensis*) so it slants slightly to create depth. Attach *Leucobryum juniperoideum* to form a round shape, effectively creating a *kokedama*. Strew white gravel around the kokedama to create color contrast and a modern air.

CHAPTER 2

River and Lake Landscapes

A Swiftly Flowing River

SCENERY FOR INSPIRATION

This work depicts a riverbank lined with ferns and swiftly-flowing water. Three types of fern are made to resemble riverside grasses, while super fine white sand is used to depict the surface foam that results from the rushing water. The texture of the shallow stone plate emphasizes the profundity of nature.

COMPOSITION

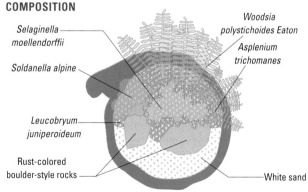

Selaginella moellendorffii

Soldanella alpine

Leucobryum juniperoideum

Rust-colored boulder-style rocks

Woodsia polystichoides Eaton

Asplenium trichomanes

White sand

Three types of fern—*Woodsia polystichoides Eaton, Asplenium trichomanes* and *Selaginella moellendorffii*—are used here, with height differences utilized to create overall balance. *Soldanella alpine* is planted to the side to resemble Japanese silver leaf (*Fargugium japonicum*) and evoke the textures of plants which grow naturally by the water. Rust-colored boulder-style rocks have been selected for the character they add to the piece, with the moss growing over their rounded, water-worn surface telling of the landscape's age.

RIVER AND LAKE LANDSCAPES ❷

A Waterfall Deep in the Mountains

SCENERY FOR INSPIRATION

In this work, the Chinese Virginia creeper (*Parthenocissus henryana*) stands in for a steep precipice, while its trailing branches resemble a waterfall. The angle at which the branches trail recalls the cool sensation of a waterfall, while the vibrant green of the leaves expresses the verdant foliage cloaking the cliffs.

COMPOSITION

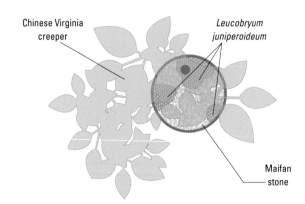

Chinese Virginia creeper

Leucobryum juniperoideum

Maifan stone

Plant the Chinese Virginia creeper in the pot working to a 7:3 ratio, covering the plant base with *Leucobryum juniperoideum* and using Maifan stones as ornamental sand. The trick here is to plant the creeper to best set off the angle of the trailing branches. As the plant grows, its leaves get larger, so prune them to complement their surroundings. You're sure to enjoy the changing colors of the leaves in the fall.

RIVER AND LAKE LANDSCAPES ❸

Fallen Leaves on the Water's Surface

SCENERY FOR INSPIRATION

The atmosphere of fallen leaves floating, swept along on the water's surface, is expressed here with a Japanese weeping maple (*Acer palmatum var. dissectum* "Inaba Shidare") for a precipice, accompanied by a pink wild rose. The trailing branches of the maple represent the leaves floating downstream.

COMPOSITION

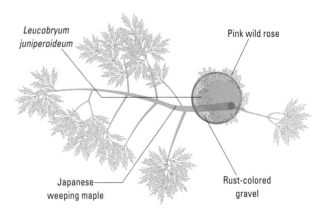

Plant the weeping maple in the pot working to a 7:3 ratio, adding in the pink wild rose at the base for the foliage to add volume. Place *Leucobryum juniperoideum* around the plants and use rust-colored gravel as ornamental sand to bring out depth. Bamboo grass or other kinds of grasses would work well in place of the pink wild rose.

Cool Branches Trailing in a Stream

SCENERY FOR INSPIRATION

The coolness of a little stream is replicated here via a bonsai of forsythia and *Sasa glabra* "Minor," with the forsythia expressing a precipice from which a tree protrudes over the stream and the *Sasa glabra* "Minor" evoking a refreshing breeze blowing over the surface of the water. The round white pot lends an air of elegance.

COMPOSITION

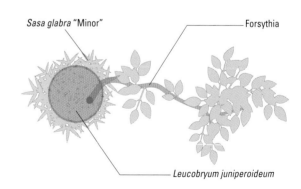

Sasa glabra "Minor" — Forsythia

Leucobryum juniperoideum

A tree growing from a clump of grass is the inspiration here, with the forsythia made to look like a precipice, and branches given a free, uncontrolled look to showcase their interesting bends. Planting miniature grass at the base of the tree has the effect of making the tree appear larger and adding depth to the work. Forsythia roots have a tendency to clump, so thin them out every 2–3 years.

Grass Swaying in the Breeze

SCENERY FOR INSPIRATION

A *Hakonechloa macra* bonsai depicts the scenery of a babbling brook along which a breeze blows, causing grasses on the banks to sway. It's the kind of brook where freshwater fish swim and fireflies can be seen. The Chinese characters for *Hakonechloa macra* are wind, knowledge and the grass that winds caress, calling to mind a cool breeze.

COMPOSITION

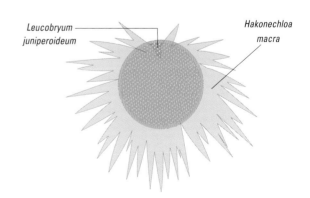

Leucobryum juniperoideum

Hakonechloa macra

Like other grasses, after more than three years of growth *Hakonechloa macra* forms an attractive shape. In order for the leaves to create a uniform roundness, make sure the plant receives sunlight from all angles. Keep watered and fertilize well. Planting *Leucobryum juniperoideum* all around the grass brings out a cool feeling.

RIVER AND LAKE LANDSCAPES ❻

A Self-Contained Habitat Miniature

SCENERY FOR INSPIRATION

This work is a snapshot of bountiful summer river scenery, hosting all kinds of flora along with creatures such as fireflies and cyprinodont fish. *Bouteloua gracilis* and *Tofieldia nuda* represent riverside grasses, the Ibigawa stones placed in an S shape express stones peeking from the water, and Yahagi sand depicts the river itself.

COMPOSITION

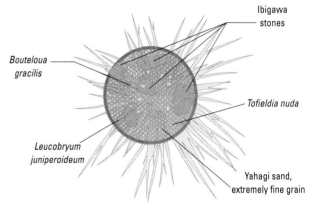

Ibigawa stones

Bouteloua gracilis

Tofieldia nuda

Leucobryum juniperoideum

Yahagi sand, extremely fine grain

Two aesthetically similar grasses, *Tofieldia nuda* and *Bouteloua gracilis* give a neat, cohesive look. The grasses have some height, so planting them in a flat pot creates atmosphere. Place large and small Ibigawa stones in an S shape to create undulations, with the ornamental sand strewn to emphasize the S shape and lend the look of a river. Small accents of moss create the look of an expanse of land in the pot.

RIVER AND LAKE LANDSCAPES ❼

A Lakeside Retreat

SCENERY FOR INSPIRATION

This work captures the attractive scenery of a lakeside spot where families come in camper vans to fish and enjoy the outdoors. Two types of hornbeam (*Carpinus*) are placed at the back of the arrangement, protruding over the rust-colored gravel strewn at the front, which represents a lake.

COMPOSITION

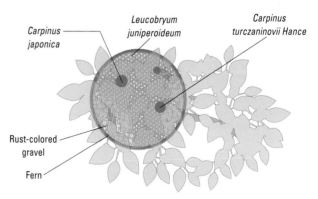

The trick to this arrangement is to get the tree leaning horizontally to resemble a tree protruding out over a lake. This requires pruning of the upward-reaching branches. By fixing the branches so that when viewed from the front, they spread out at a 45 degree angle, space opens up at the front and depth is created. Plant a fern at the base and use *Leucobryum juniperoideum* to soften the borders between the gravel and the trees.

CHAPTER 3

Forest Landscapes

FOREST LANDSCAPES ❶
A Peaceful Conifer Forest

SCENERY FOR INSPIRATION

Here, a bonsai landscape depicts a forest of needle-leaved trees through which cool air wafts. Showing some of the bark on the trunk of the Japanese cypress builds the sense of aged trees. Ibigawa stones represent rocky outcrops throughout the forest, while ornamental Kurama sand stands in for the fallen leaves which have turned brown as they lie on the ground.

COMPOSITION

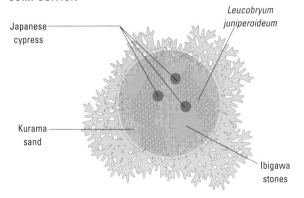

Plant multiple Japanese cypresses (here, three have been used) to form a scalene triangle when viewed from above. Balance *Leucobryum juniperoideum* plantings with Ibigawa stones at the base of the trees. Trim the lower branches to reveal bark on the trunks, creating the authentic look of a forest of needle-leaved trees. When a tree by itself appears insufficient, plant several together to fill in space and create a natural look.

Little Pieces of Nature Beside a Mountain Path

SCENERY FOR INSPIRATION

This work highlights the small plants growing at the sides of mountain paths used for hiking. They're easy to miss, but if you look closely, little weeds are brilliantly colored and uniquely shaped. This sentiment is expressed in this bonsai.

COMPOSITION

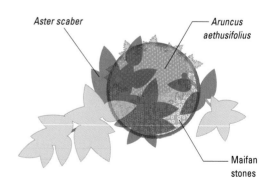

Aster scaber

Aruncus aethusifolius

Maifan stones

Plant *Aster scaber* and *Aruncus aethusifolius* together in a pot and allow them to mature. After the third year, both plants will have filled out to a good size and will look natural. Make sure to maintain the *Aster scaber* to bring out differences in height. As it's a tall plant, use a short, outspreading pot for a stabilizing effect.

Morning Sun Streaming Through the Trees

SCENERY FOR INSPIRATION

Here, two plantings of Amur maple (*Acer japonicum*) form one bonsai, recalling nature's warmth in the form of a mountain's bounties found when gathering mushrooms, mountain vegetables and the like. The two pots placed together evoke the scenery of a forest continuing into the distance.

COMPOSITION

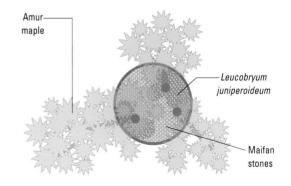

Amur maple

Leucobryum juniperoideum

Maifan stones

Plant multiple Amur maple trees (here, three have been used) of different statures to form a scalene triangle in the pot when viewed from above. Consider the trees' stature to create a balanced arrangement, planting a tall, medium and short tree to face various directions so that their branches do not overlap. Place *Leucobryum juniperoideum* over the base and use Maifan stones as ornamental sand to represent a path.

Budding Plants on
the Forest Floor

SCENERY FOR INSPIRATION

This piece describes a tree striving to reach the single shaft of light that pierces through the canopy, after having sprouted in the mountains from a seed a bird has dropped. The charming leaves of the Amur Maple (*Acer japonicum)* and the beauty of its branches express the loveliness of plants.

COMPOSITION

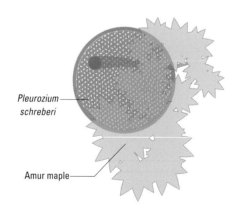

Pleurozium schreberi

Amur maple

As this planting incorporates only one tree, a significant amount of space can be used to accommodate the slant of its branches, with the tree planted at a 7:3 ratio in the pot. An attractive result is achieved if the branches protrude from the pot at a 5:5 ratio. Plant *Pleurozium schreberi* around the tree to bring out a natural look.

A Dense, Dark Forest

SCENERY FOR INSPIRATION

Depicting a little-visited, dense forest of various types of trees, this bonsai brings together a *Premna japonica* and *Selaginella moellendorffii*. When it comes to maintaining the *Premna japonica*, exercise restraint, allowing some parts to grow out to achieve an air of rich rural beauty.

COMPOSITION

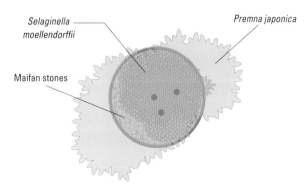

Selaginella moellendorffii

Premna japonica

Maifan stones

Position the *Premna japonica* at the back of the arrangement with the *Selaginella moellendorffii* at the front, planted to grow in a rounded shape. Planting the tree at the back creates the impression of approaching greenery. Two years or so after planting, the *Premna japonica* and *Selaginella moellendorffii* should start to form a coherent composition. The *Premna japonica* is known as the musk maple, and as the name suggests, gives off a strong odor that repels insect pests.

FOREST LANDSCAPES ❻

A Beech Tree Peeks Through Bamboo

SCENERY FOR INSPIRATION

This piece depicts the scenery of a beech tree (*Fagus crenata*) that has sprouted from a seed carried into a dense, ground-covering thicket of bamboo grass. Allowing the fine leaves of *Arundinariinae* to take over the whole pot evokes the ever-reaching vitality of plant life.

COMPOSITION

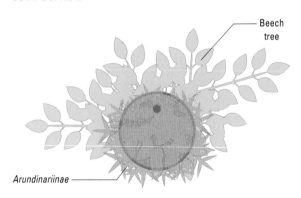

Beech tree

Arundinariinae

Position the beech at the back of the arrangement and the *Arundinariinae* in front at its base. *Arundinariinae* is one of the smallest bamboo grasses and has fine leaves, making plants it accompanies look larger and lending perspective to a composition. Allow three years for it to fill out in the pot and make sure to train it into an attractive shape. Take care not to let the beech dry out.

FOREST LANDSCAPES ❼

Splendid Hillside Foliage

SCENERY FOR INSPIRATION

Here, a bonsai of Chinese fringe flower (*Loropetalum chinense*) portrays the hills clad in fall colors. The leaves turning red, green and purple express the activity in the mountains, while the tree form depicts a precipice jutting out over water.

COMPOSITION

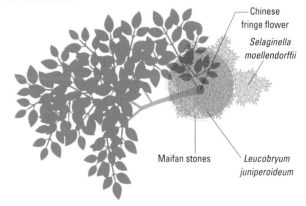

Chinese fringe flower

Selaginella moellendorffii

Maifan stones

Leucobryum juniperoideum

Plant the Chinese fringe flower in the pot working to a 7:3 ratio with *Selaginella moellendorffii* at its base and *Leucobryum juniperoideum* as a ground cover. Use Maifan stones as ornamental sand to achieve an elegant look in the white pot. Train the tree so the branches hang towards the front of the arrangement, working so that the branches and the pot are on a ratio of about 7:3 and pruning any branches that grow straight up.

A Big Tree in a Sunlit Park

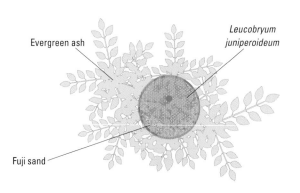

SCENERY FOR INSPIRATION

A bonsai of evergreen ash (*Fraxinus griffithii*) portrays a large tree taking in the strong rays of summer sun in the urban oasis of a park. The glossy leaves of the ash replicate sunlight.

COMPOSITION

Evergreen ash

Leucobryum juniperoideum

Fuji sand

The shrubby evergreen ash is trained into a fan shape—the trick to achieving a beautiful result is to prune off any extraneous branches for a clean look. Plant moss around the tree to form an attractive roundness, with Fuji sand used for decoration. The color contrast of the green plant and moss, the black sand and the white pot makes for a modern impression.

A Bamboo Forest Path Leading to a Temple

SCENERY FOR INSPIRATION

Horsetail *(Equisetum hyemale)* stands in for bamboo in this arrangement depicting a path in a bamboo forest in the grounds of an ancient city's temple. The rounded, gently sloping hills of moss are intended to create the impression of stepping into a fairytale world.

COMPOSITION

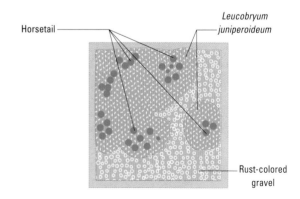

Horsetail

Leucobryum juniperoideum

Rust-colored gravel

In a rectangular tin pot, form mountains of varying sizes, using clay soil to create a framework with undulations and a compost in which to plant the horsetail. The mountains should be slightly triangular in shape, while the horsetail should fan out a little to give the impression of an expanse of space and create an attractive appearance. Use rust-colored gravel as ornamental sand to form a path.

A Lush, Verdant Bamboo Grove

SCENERY FOR INSPIRATION

Horsetail (*Equisetum prealtum*) represents bamboo in this arrangement which expresses the refreshing breeziness of a bamboo forest. Planting *Leucobryum juniperoideum* around the horsetail and using a black pot to make the composition appear more compact convey a sense of the bamboo forest's expanse and highlights the vibrancy of the greenery.

COMPOSITION

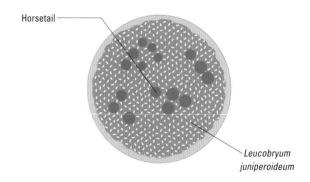

Horsetail

Leucobryum juniperoideum

As horsetail is straight and grows vertically, it's important to plant it perpendicular to the pot and in equal amounts on both sides so that its stems don't overlap. There are multiple stands of plants in the one pot here, each positioned at a 7:3 ratio to the pot and planted to match the stand in the center for a natural-looking result.

A Summer Resort with a Pleasant, Cool Breeze

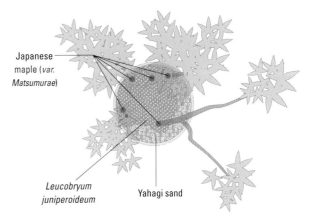

SCENERY FOR INSPIRATION

A bonsai of Japanese maple (*Acer palmatum var. Matsumurae*) portrays the kind of open space at a summer resort where white birches grow. The coolness of the passing breeze in the fresh light of a summer morning is expressed here via the green leaves of the maple and the turquoise blue glaze of the pot.

COMPOSITION

Japanese maple (*var. Matsumurae*)

Leucobryum juniperoideum

Yahagi sand

Arrange multiple maple trees (here, five have been used) so the branches do not cross and so the composition is balanced. Allow space between the roots when planting to create a refreshing impression. Use trees of different height, with one tall tree, two medium and two smaller trees for variation and to lend an air of expanse to the arrangement.

A Well-Tended Park

SCENERY FOR INSPIRATION

This arrangement symbolizes the scenery of an urban park where families enjoy spending days off, with *Zelkova* representing the trees in the park and ornamental Kurama sand used to sketch out a path. It captures the feeling of a place where nature can be enjoyed fully and safely under dappled sunlight.

COMPOSITION

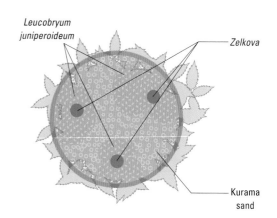

Leucobryum juniperoideum

Zelkova

Kurama sand

Three *Zelkova* trees of tall, medium and short stature are planted so as to be in scalene triangle formation when viewed from overhead. Variations in the trees' height lend distance to the arrangement. *Leucobryum juniperoideum* is planted at the base of the trees, interspersed with ornamental Kurama sand. Train the trees so that the trunks are visible and the foliage grows to form a round shape.

CHAPTER 4

Ocean View Landscapes

A Hilly Promontory with Sea Breezes

SCENERY FOR INSPIRATION

This piece shows the scenery of gently sloping hills extending over a promontory. The Ezo spruce trees (*Picea jezoensis*) are planted to all slant the same way to indicate the strength of the sea breeze, with the scraggy Ibigawa stones representing cliffs and white ornamental sand for the sea.

COMPOSITION

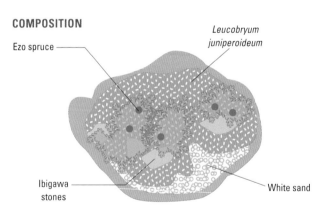

Use clay soil to form a framework, then pour in compost to form mountains of various sizes. Plant five Ezo spruces together to form the composition, with three on the large mountain and two on the small mountain to create variation in height. Create a path between the large and small mountains with the air of a pleasant walking trail. Position Ibigawa stones of various sizes in the composition and cover them with *Leucobryum juniperoideum*.

A Lone Pine on a Rugged Precipice

SCENERY FOR INSPIRATION

The landscape of a pine tree surviving through years of wind and snow on a steep cliff, after having been carried there as a seed on the sea breeze is expressed in this red pine (*Pinus densiflora*) bonsai. The courage and beauty of a plant living in such a harsh environment is highlighted in this literati bonsai style.

COMPOSITION

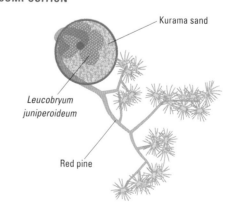

Kurama sand

Leucobryum juniperoideum

Red pine

Position a literati style red pine so that the trunk is on an angle leaning towards the pot and so that the ratio of space in the pot is 7:3. Adjust the tree so that the branches and the pot are also balanced at a ratio of 7:3. Interesting branch formations characterize the literati style, so make sure they are shown to best effect. Plant *Leucobryum juniperoideum* at the base to create undulations and use Kurama sand for decoration.

Clumps of Grass
Behind a Beach

SCENERY FOR INSPIRATION

At the end of a small path is a vast expanse of summer coast-line. The fine leaves of *Miscanthus sinensis f. gracillimus* resemble summer grasses, while the beach that can be seen when the clumps of grass are parted is expressed via rust-colored gravel. It's a piece that suggests a sandy beach and blue sea.

COMPOSITION

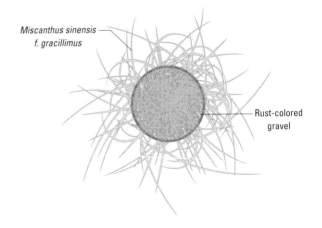

Miscanthus sinensis
f. gracillimus

Rust-colored
gravel

Plant the grasses together, allowing the foliage to thicken and form a fan shape. Grasses begin to take on a natural look after three years, so think ahead and take good care of the plants in the first and second years. It's crucial to make sure they don't dry out and are kept well fertilized.

A Tropical Resort

SCENERY FOR INSPIRATION

The scenery of a tropical resort with an open field of view in all directions is expressed here via wax trees (*Toxicoden-dron succedaneum* or *Rhus succedanea*). Trained into simple shapes, with their few branches the wax trees appear like palm trees dotted across the landscape.

COMPOSITION

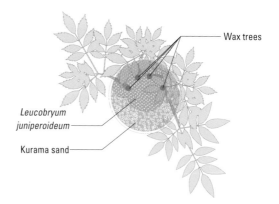

Plant the wax trees with their few branches together, training them so the upper leaves spread out in a fan formation. Use as many trees as is necessary to fill in any space that seems empty. Spread *Leucobryum juniperoideum* over the base and complete the composition with Kurama sand for decoration. As it's a member of the sumac family, its lacquer may cause an allergic reaction, so take care during maintenance of these trees.

The Tropics Where Ficus Trees Grow

SCENERY FOR INSPIRATION

Here, a typical tropical island landscape where huge ficus retusa trees grow aerial roots from their branches is expressed via a *Serissa japonica* with exposed roots. The single blossom serves to further highlight the tropical air.

COMPOSITION

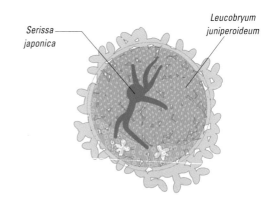

Serissa
japonica

Leucobryum
juniperoideum

Exposed roots are created by bringing the roots out to above the surface to cause lignification. It's a good idea to prune off extraneous branches sprouting from the roots at this time. The variation between the roots, trunk and leaves creates balance. *Serissa japonica* is a perennial that flowers several times a year and lends itself to being pruned into various shapes.

The Sea Around Matsushima Island

SCENERY FOR INSPIRATION

This work captures the scenery of Matsushima, where pine trees have taken root on small islands bobbing in the ocean. The islands are expressed in the roundness of the moss, with ornamental Yahagi sand representing the ocean. Position the soil and ornamental sand deep down to add depth to the shadows.

COMPOSITION

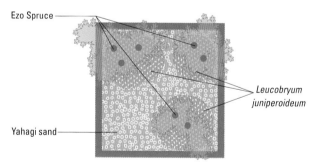

Ezo Spruce

Leucobryum juniperoideum

Yahagi sand

In a square Shigaraki ware ceramic pot, use clay soil to build up the foundation and create three mountains. Separating out the space between the mountains creates an entrance and exit, engendering a feeling of depth. Using clay soil to stabilize the composition prevents soil being washed away when watering. Plant multiple Ezo spruce (*Picea jezoensis*) trees (here, seven have been used) to create the composition, with trees of roughly the same height in groups of three, two and two over the three mountains. I was keeping in mind how to create perspective, depth and space when completing this piece.

CHAPTER 5
Other Landscapes

The Vivid Color of Old Maple Trees

SCENERY FOR INSPIRATION

This bonsai depicts the vibrant colors of a Japanese maple standing in a corner of a temple in an ancient city. The atmosphere and spirituality of the Buddhist temple are expressed in the elegantly trailing branches of the *Acer palmatum Dissectum* "Inaba Shidare." The form of its long, delicate leaves and the red that colors even its branches are a joy to behold.

COMPOSITION

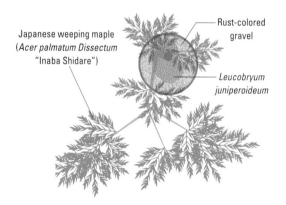

Japanese weeping maple (*Acer palmatum Dissectum* "Inaba Shidare")

Rust-colored gravel

Leucobryum juniperoideum

Plant the maple at a 7:3 ratio in the pot to maximize the amount of space beneath the branches that forms because of the direction in which they are trailing. At the same time, make sure the branches extending from the pot are at a 7:3 ratio. Place *Leucobryum juniperoideum* around the base and strew rust-colored gravel over it to bring out a refined look.

A Meticulously Manicured Japanese Garden

SCENERY FOR INSPIRATION

A beautifully maintained pine in a traditional Japanese garden is represented here via a Japanese white pine (*Pinus parviflora*) in the informal upright style of bonsai. The Ibigawa stones positioned flat on the ground suggest a Japanese rock garden, while the turquoise blue glaze of the pot lends the look of a pond landscape.

COMPOSITION

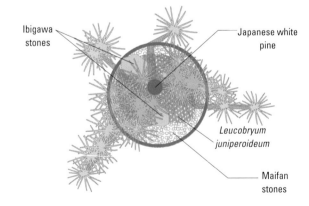

Ibigawa stones

Japanese white pine

Leucobryum juniperoideum

Maifan stones

The trunk describes an S shape in this orthodox informal upright style bonsai, which is trained to taper from the base upwards. Maintenance and training of the branches is crucial in order to achieve the triangle formation. Position three Ibigawa stones at the base and plant *Leucobryum juniperoideum* between them. Using a shallow, flat pot lends a greater sense of stability to the composition.

A Massive Christmas Tree

SCENERY FOR INSPIRATION

This work recalls the giant Christmas trees that are displayed in famous places. Japanese firs (*Abies firma*) can reach a height of 30 feet (10 meters) or more. Here, a Japanese cypress gives the impression of a grandeur in a small pot.

COMPOSITION

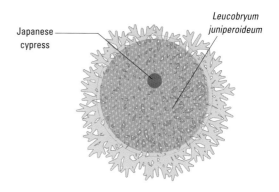

Japanese cypress

Leucobryum juniperoideum

As this is a single tree with a straight trunk growing upright, plant it in the center of the pot, with *Leucobryum juniperoideum* spread around the base. To achieve the attractive cone shape, decide on the outline and prune back the branches and leaves that protrude from it, viewing the tree from all angles to check the form of the cone. Use your fingers, not scissors, to prune the tree. Make sure to frequently remove the dead leaves from the center to ensure good ventilation.

OTHER LANDSCAPES ❹

A Turtle with a Moss-Covered Carapace

SCENERY FOR INSPIRATION

This work symbolizes the understated beauty of a tortoise whose carapace has become covered with moss over the years. The tortoise container is a bronze casting (design: Yuriko Aoki; production: Nousaku). The texture of the bronze works well with the color of the moss.

COMPOSITION

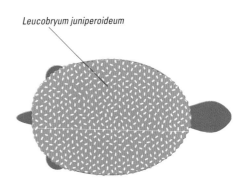

Leucobryum juniperoideum

There is no hole in the base of the container, so spread root rot inhibitor over the base before adding clay soil and covering it with *Leucobryum juniperoideum*. Keep the finished work in a spot with dappled sunlight and good ventilation. Make sure it gets a reasonable amount of water and that it doesn't get moldy.

OTHER LANDSCAPES ❺

A Moss Hedgehog

SCENERY FOR INSPIRATION

Image © Shi-iku Gakari

In this piece, moss is used to resemble a hedgehog's needles. The hedgehog container is a bronze casting (design: Yuriko Aoki; production: Nousaku). Use *Leucobryum bowringii Mitt.* to bring out the look of hedgehog spines.

COMPOSITION

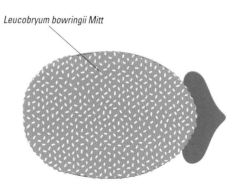

Leucobryum bowringii Mitt

There is no hole in the base of the container, so spread root rot inhibitor over the base before adding clay soil and covering it with *Leucobryum juniperoideum.* If kept indoors, the moss may go moldy and die, so keep the finished work in a spot with good ventilation and make sure it doesn't dry out.

A Flock of Sheep Awaiting Shearing

SCENERY FOR INSPIRATION

This work depicts sheep gathering into a flock while awaiting shearing on a sheep farm. The figure of the five sheep lined up together is adorable, with the moss resembling their wool.

COMPOSITION

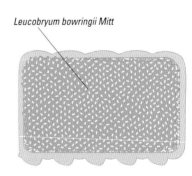

Leucobryum bowringii Mitt

There is no hole in the base of this cast brass container (design: Yuriko Aoki; production: Nousaku), so spread root rot inhibitor over the bottom before piling in clay soil and covering it with *Leucobryum bowringii Mitt*. To enhance the appearance of sheep herding together, create shallow undulations. Keep the finished work in a humid place with good ventilation to grow the moss attractively.

PART TWO
Bonsai Landscapes

Your original bonsai landscape is the only one like it in the whole world, and you've worked hard to create it. So rather than just sticking it on a shelf, you'll want to display it as attractively as possible. This section introduces the accoutrements that enhance bonsai landscapes and techniques to display them more effectively in various situations.

About Accoutrements

Accoutrements are objects such as decorations and furnishings that fit out a space for a particular situation. In Japan, the word for accoutrement (shitsurai) takes its meaning from fitting out a display alcove, entrance foyer or other room (shitsu) with the decorations for seasonal events and turning points in life to get us into the spirit of the occasion. The accoutrements used for bonsai landscapes are intended for indoor use in spaces such as display alcoves. Taking particular care to choose the right setting for your landscape allows for deeper appreciation of impermanence in nature, and of the beauty of the bonsai and the changes in the seasons.

Just as bonsai are plants whose beauty is formed by human hands, containers made from natural substances become enticing when transformed by the human touch. For example, we are drawn to vessels made from wood, steel, stone and so on that are engineered to show their inherent characteristics to advantage. Containers like these allow us to enjoy the full impact of bonsai even if our homes have no real dedicated display space, and regardless of whether our interior style is Japanese or western. On these pages are some of the accoutrements used at my company, Sinajina, in Tokyo.

Plates made of tin (left) and brass (right). (Production: Nousaku) Introducing opulent colors as accents is ideal for creating a sophisticated space.

Oblongs of Yakijime unglazed earthenware (large, medium, small). The chic shade draws out the vibrancy of the bonsai. These allow the use of space to be restricted.

Shallow stone plate. The stone has an attractive texture and a rustic look. Paired with grasses, it highlights the delicacy of the leaves.

Rusted steel display stand. (Production: Iwashimizu Kyu) The modern shape fits in perfectly with today's lifestyle, while the rusting steel provides a contrast to the vitality of greenery.

Hou-sa, dark. (Construction: Shimoo Design) Simple shapes and classic colors convey a sense of luxury. The name Hou-sa comes from "hou," which means a square or oblong shape, and "sa," which indicates nature. This piece is designed with the notion that shapes from nature are beautiful as they are.

Hou-sa, clear. (Construction: Shimoo Design) The natural shade of this floor stand enhances the greenery of the bonsai. Shapes like these Hou-sa can be found in different sizes for a beautifully balanced landscape.

Fossil wood. (Construction: Shimoo Design) This floor stand made of Japanese ash has an attractive grain. Its height creates just the right amount of empty space.

Long octagonal plate. (Construction: Shimoo Design) This display board is easy to use in arrangements, and is defined by the way it develops character over years of use.

Thick circular plate (left); hexagonal plate (right). (Construction: Shimoo Design) The simple shapes and natural appearance are attractive and are an easy fit for almost any setting.

Examples of Their Use in Displays

How to Display Your Bonsai

When arranging bonsai for display, it's important to create a balanced layout by placing the elements according to the shape and form of both the accoutrements and the bonsai. When aiming for balance, dividing the accoutrements and the bonsai into categories makes things easier. Round and square accoutrements are "static," while rectangular and other altered shapes are "dynamic." In the same way, trees that grow straight and vertical are "static," whereas those with slanted trunks or with weeping branches and other kinds of movement are "dynamic."

There are four ways of combining bonsai and their accoutrements: static + static; static + dynamic; dynamic + static and dynamic + dynamic. In order to achieve overall balance it's important to keep these combinations in mind. Here, we examine some good examples of the four display combinations.

Displaying Static Accoutrements with Static Bonsai

An example of an upright bonsai displayed on a square piece of indigo dyed fabric. Placing the bonsai in the very center results in an air of stability.

An example of an upright bonsai displayed on a round tin plate which in turn rests on a round timber plate. The bonsai is placed in the very center of the two layers of plates.

Displaying Static Accoutrements with Dynamic Bonsai

An example of a dynamic bonsai displayed on a square plate. Placing the pot in the center of the plate results in an air of stability.

An example of a dynamic bonsai displayed on a round tin plate. Placing the pot in the center of the plate creates the right balance.

Displaying Dynamic Accoutrements with Static Bonsai

An example of an upright bonsai displayed on an oblong floor stand. Divide the stand into tenths and place the bonsai at the 3/10 mark.

An example of an upright bonsai displayed on an irregularly shaped rusted steel ornamental board. Placing the bonsai about 3/10 of the way along the board results in a balanced look.

Displaying Dynamic Accoutrements with Dynamic Bonsai

An example of a slanted style bonsai displayed on an oblong floor stand. Place the bonsai 3/10 of the way along, opening up space between the bonsai's trunk and the longer section of the board.

An example of two oblong display boards placed together for exhibiting bonsai. Place the bonsai about 3/10 of the way in from where the boards meet, opening up space in the direction that the bonsai is leaning.

Examples of Badly Balanced Displays

This is an example of a poor display of dynamic accoutrements and a dynamic bonsai. The trunk is leaning away from the display and the pot is set only 2/10 in from the end of the board, meaning there is no sense of stability. Make sure to open up space within the display in the direction the branches are flowing and to place the bonsai 3/10 from the end of the board.

This is an example of a poor display of static accoutrements and a dynamic bonsai. When the bonsai is off-center on the board, it gives the impression of instability. Make sure the bonsai is placed in the very center of the board.

Enjoying an alcove.

Delighting in curves against a
backdrop of man-made lines.

A refreshing forest in a Japanese-style room.

Grasses enact a cool summer breeze.

59

A place for greetings and goodbyes
with a feel of dappled sunlight.

Greenery that merges into a living space.

Refreshing greenery by a window.

Tea time in the shade of trees.

A moment of supreme bliss.

Snapshot of a breezy grass plain.

PART THREE

Using Everyday Containers

Normally, bonsai landscapes are created in special purpose-made pots. However, it's possible to use everyday items to house your bonsai. It can be a special way to use things to which you have a certain attachment and can't bring yourself to throw out. To transform them into pots, it'll be necessary to add drainage holes. In this section, we'll look at how to make holes in everyday containers and show you some of these transformations, and the types of bonsai creations that suit them.

Modifying Everyday Containers for Bonsai

Bonsai pots are produced with plant care and compatibility in mind, so normally, it's advisable to plant bonsai in these specialized pots. However, everyday containers of all kinds can be turned into pots. Here, we introduce examples of everyday bits and pieces used in bonsai landscapes—favorite sundry items, wedding presents that have gone unused, cooking utensils that are suitable when you're living alone but don't work when you're sharing your living space, and so on. Since the average household container doesn't have drainage holes, you'll need to add them. It's also important to be sure that the container and the plant are compatible and work together from a design perspective, so that the effect looks artful and deliberate, not makeshift. The more commonplace the item, the harder it is to transform into a bonsai, but for those who want to try making bonsai from items at hand, these are the basics.

Everyday items used in this section

Coffee dripper

Tin canister

Teapot

Milk pan

Candle

Ash tray

Wooden sake cup

Soap dish

Cup for soba soup

Small bowl

How to Make Holes in Containers

Adding a drainage hole to the base of a repurposed container helps maintain your plants' health. Use an electric drill to create a hole in the center of the base about ⅜ inch (1 cm) in diameter. If it's not practical to make a hole in the center of the base, there are alternatives, such as making three holes equidistant from the edge of the base. The main thing is to make sure that water can drain from the pot, so once you have made the hole, pour water into the container and check whether it's draining out properly. If for some reason it's impossible to make a hole in the container, use Seramis granules (see soils, p86) instead of regular soil to prevent root rot.

Items Required for Making Holes

Electric drill
*The size of the hole can be adjusted depending on the size of the drill attachment. Use a size suitable for the pot.

Small bowl
This store-bought little bowl serves as a sample for making holes.

Aluminum wire
Used to secure net over the drainage hole.

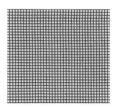

Netting for the base
Plastic netting to place over the hole in the base of the pot.

1. Turn the pot upside down and spray water over it using a spray bottle. Direct the electric drill at the point where the hole will be and start chipping into the pot.

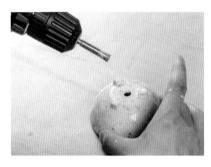

2. Check the size of the hole.

3. Cut the net to match the size of the hole, then form a U shape from a suitable length of aluminum wire and pass it through the net.

4. Bring the aluminum wire from the inside of the pot through the net and out of the hole in the base.

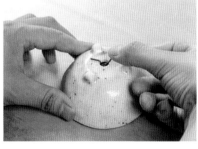

5. Bend the aluminum wire out to both sides, securing the net to finish preparing the pot.

6. Making a hole in the base and covering it with net works for a lot of different types of containers.

A black pine planted in a small bowl meant
as tableware creates a contemporary feel.

Japanese andromeda, Japanese spirea and white willow planted
together create a western style bonsai arrangement.

There's no need to make a hole in a coffee dripper. The dripper below houses a cherry tree.

Rock and pine in an antique ashtray.

Gardening sensibilities match *Rhodotypos* and *Sisyrinchium rosulatum* in a tin container.

A fresh young *Woodsia polystichoides Eaton* is perfect planted in a wooden sake cup.

東北に酒・あり
蛍川
エイ
セン

Japanese maple (*Acer palmatum var. Matsumurae*) and a kokedama of *Ophiopogon japonicus Ker.f.nanus fort* lend a refined air to a soap dish.

A Virginia creeper that cascades from cliffs is paired with a candle.

Planted in a teapot, a *Vaccinium oldhamii* with magnificent branches makes for an avant-garde piece.

A Tsuyama cypress planted in a little cup for soba soup.

PART FOUR

Outdoor Bonsai Landscape Ideas

Bonsai landscapes allow greenery to be incorporated into everyday living. Even in an urban home or apartment, which may have little or no garden space, you can create a landscape in a pot and enjoy the greenery. If you have a little plot, dead space, veranda or any other kind of space, however small, you can incorporate greenery into it in ways that support your ideas for bonsai landscapes. In this section, we will introduce some of the examples of construction that Sinajina has developed for adapting spaces to suit this purpose.

Working with a Limited Space

This construction example shows a way to enhance a long narrow area. On the long approach to the house, concrete containing charcoal has been used. This is attractive when wet and sets off the green of the plantings, making for a design that lifts the mood especially on rainy days, which can tend to be gloomy. In the courtyard garden a stone washbasin has been installed along with stepping stones to create the look of a tea ceremony garden for the enjoyment of the client's wife, as she practices the art of tea.

Design: LEVEL Architects

Making Use of a Veranda

A garden in the image of a giant kokedama has been created in the limited space of a veranda. As it is artificial ground, care was needed with regard to drainage and weighting. Lengths of white and rust-colored granite and concrete blocks are positioned to create balance, adding playful touches of line and color. Evergreens such as *Symplocos prunifolia* are used as the main trees, with deciduous *Lindera umbellata* for interest, creating a space where greenery can be enjoyed. The overall design is neither Japanese nor western in order to complement the modern house.

Utilizing an Existing Garden Space 1

The draw of this apartment is its ground floor garden—a functional garden that allows for appreciation of the four seasons. Evergreens such as *Symplocos prunifolia* and red and white flowering camellia that grow even in shaded areas form the main planting. To enhance the pleasure of stepping into the garden, the stonemason carefully selected each stone when creating the path along the corridor that leads outdoors.

Utilizing an Existing Garden Space 2

Client M in Ota ward

This example shows how a garden with the appearance of an upscale property that's been handed down over generations has been utilized in creating a moss garden. The main garden, courtyard and approach to the house were all landscaped by a renowned garden designer, but the simple and modern *Dicranum scoparium Heds.* moss garden was designed to play up the feel of the existing garden while making it low maintenance to suit today's lifestyle. Undulating moss and gravel have been used along the approach to the house, with care taken to create a pleasing landscape and a feeling of depth even in a narrow space.

Utilizing an Existing Garden Space 3

Client Y in Meguro ward

Working from the concept of adding another room to this ground floor apartment, we created a laid-back garden that makes going outside enjoyable. A deck large enough for an adult to lie on was added to the veranda, with antique Oya tuff stone tiles laid on the ground adding atmosphere.

Utilizing an Existing Garden Space 4

While this garden's existing components were good, it had become overgrown, so we transformed it into a low-maintenance moss garden. Planted with *Dicranum scoparium Heds.*, it's designed as a garden to enjoy showing to others. The existing plants were utilized, with plants that convey a sense of the seasons added, such as *Acer palmatum var. Matsumurae*.

Making Use of a Sunken Space

We created a rock garden-style garden in the dry area adjoining the semi-basement at Yasaiya Mei, a restaurant belonging Akira Watanabe, former executive chef at Global Dining and CEO of eatwalk. As the area is below ground level, evergreen plants that can grow in the shade such as *Symplocos prunifolia* were planted, along with seasonal grasses. Large steel pots in three different sizes and rough-hewn rocks were used bring out depth and create atmosphere.

PART FIVE
Basic Information

Naturally, bonsai landscaping calls for pots, tools, soils and other materials used in bonsai gardening. Equally important, you will need to know how to use these things to create bonsai landscapes. Knowledge about bonsai maintenance is also invaluable in order to enjoy the piece you worked so hard to create for many years to come. This section is a summary of the basic knowledge needed to create and maintain bonsai landscapes.

Tools

First of all, assemble the basic tools needed for making bonsai landscapes. There are various types of bonsai tools for different purposes, and these are sold at specialist stores, gardening stores, home centers and so on. Here, we introduce the basic tools. Firstly, you will need bonsai scissors to prune branches and so on, tweezers with a spatula attached for smoothing soil, chopsticks and a spray bottle. Apart from these, prepare a scoop for pouring in soil, net to place over the base of pots, and aluminum wire to hold the net in place. A hand broom and a tub or bucket are also handy.

Basic Tools

Bonsai scissors
Used for trimming roots and branches. Gardening scissors for cutting flowers make a good substitute.

Tweezers with spatula attached
Used for teasing out roots, nipping off fine foliage and removing insects. The spatula section is handy for neatening soil, ornamental sand and so on.

Rake
The rake at the end of this spatula can be used for teasing out roots of bonsai that are larger than the shohin (palm) size.

Rounded chopstick
Bamboo chopsticks are used for pressing moss down onto soil or pressing soil into the gaps between roots when planting.

Spray bottle
A spray bottle is used for watering and for settling the soil after planting. The fitted nozzle allows mist to reach tight spots. Look for the type that can spray even when tilted on an angle.

Scoop
Used for pouring in stones to line the base of a pot or pouring in soil. In particular, prevents spilling when pouring soil into a pot.

Hand broom
A hand broom is useful for sweeping up soil around a work platform.

Aluminum wire
Used as wire for training bonsai and to secure net at the base of a pot.

Netting for the base of pots
Plastic netting is used to cover the hole inside pots. It prevents soil spilling out of the hole and allows water to drain out. It also prevents insect infestations.

Other scissors
Apart from basic tools, there are also specialist bonsai scissors. These are particularly recommended for those who intend to take up bonsai seriously.

Stainless steel scissors
As these are stainless and unlikely to rust, they are recommended for beginners and for people using them infrequently.

Azalea scissors
These scissors are used for pruning delicate foliage. As they are used for delicate work, the tips are finely pointed.

Italian pruning shears
These have hand grips and operate using springs, so can be used for a long time without tiring hands.

Branch cutters
These are used to cut shoots that emerge from between branches or to thin out branches. Plants recover quickly when cut using these.

Design scissors
These are not cast—they are made by hand by artisans who hammer steel to create custom-made items.

Bonsai Pots

The "bon" part of the word bonsai indicates the pot, which is the plant's home as well as the attire that enhances its appearance. For this reason, selecting pots is extremely important. Bonsai pots are available in all kinds of shapes, colors and materials, and the overall look of the bonsai changes completely depending on the pot chosen. Visualizing the type of pot in which to plant a tree is one of the pleasures of creating bonsai. Take your time choosing the pot, keeping in mind the overall balance it creates with the plant, where it will be displayed and so on. Here, we introduce some of the bonsai pots stocked at Sinajina.

Round earthenware pots (white) by Sinajina. Pots of this shape generally come in multiple sizes. White sets off plants' vivid color, making it suitable for various types of plants. Simple, modern pots like these work with contemporary decor regardless of whether that decor is Japanese or western in style.

Round earthenware pots (black) by Sinajina. Like the white of the pots above, black also brings out the vividness of the plants and the scenery created within the pot, lending a modern air.

Shallow earthenware pots (large, medium and small) by Sinajina. Pots that are low in height serve to make trees look bigger and enhance the appearance of landscapes created within them.

Round glazed pots (artist: Nobuhiko Tanaka). (Left) Bronze. (Right) Turquoise blue. The bronze shade has warmth to it, while the turquoise blue has an air of coolness, allowing the pots to be paired with plants to express a sense of the seasons.

(Left) Round tin pot. (Right) Round brass pot. (Production: Nousaku). The tin pot looks cool and refreshing, while the brass pot is perfect for expressing glamor. They are well suited for growing plants and give off an air of uniqueness.

Soils to Use in Bonsai Landscapes

The soil that is best suited for bonsai landscapes is uncontaminated, drains well but remains hydrated and does not clot. Here, we introduce bonsai soils that meet these conditions. Generally, rather than using one single type, several kinds of soil are blended together for use in bonsai.

Akadama soil
This red volcanic soil has long been a major component of bonsai cultivation. The granules are hard and excellent at retaining fertilizer and water while also providing good drainage and air circulation, making Akadama the most suitable basic soil for bonsai.

Clay soil
This clay type of soil is formed through the humification of sediment composed of reeds, wild rice and other plants that grow in swampy areas. It is highly viscous and doesn't crumble easily. It hardens when dry, so can be used as an adhesive agent in kokedama and when attaching rocks.

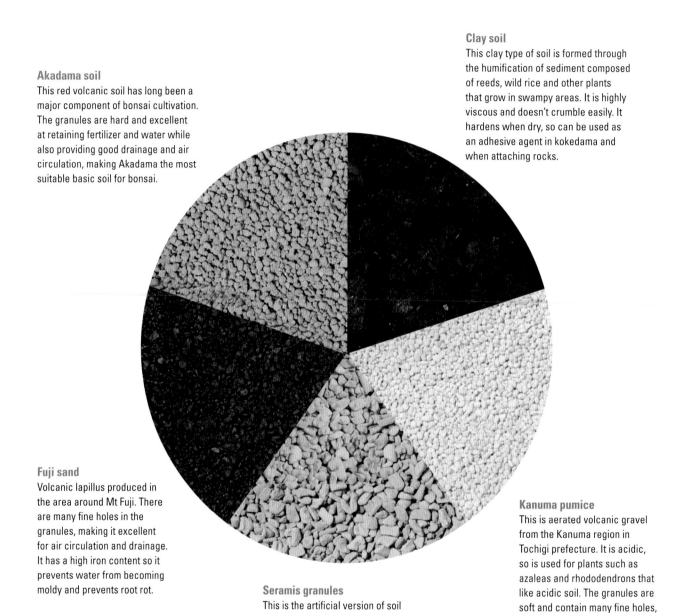

Fuji sand
Volcanic lapillus produced in the area around Mt Fuji. There are many fine holes in the granules, making it excellent for air circulation and drainage. It has a high iron content so it prevents water from becoming moldy and prevents root rot.

Seramis granules
This is the artificial version of soil produced in the German mountain region of Westerwald. It has excellent drainage properties and does not rot or decompose, so is used to prevent root rot when growing bonsai in containers without holes.

Kanuma pumice
This is aerated volcanic gravel from the Kanuma region in Tochigi prefecture. It is acidic, so is used for plants such as azaleas and rhododendrons that like acidic soil. The granules are soft and contain many fine holes, making it excellent for air circulation and water retention.

Ornamental Sand and Stones

Ornamental Sand

Ornamental sand is the sand strewn over the top of the soil to enhance the appearance of the plants and landscape—makeup, in a sense. It can change the mood of a bonsai and be used to represent bodies of water such as the ocean, rivers and lakes as well as roads. There is also a technique that involves using coarse ornamental sand to express scenery that's local, and using a fine-grain type to express the scenery of faraway places. Here, we introduce some different types of ornamental sand. If these specific sands aren't available to you, substitute sands of similar textures and colors.

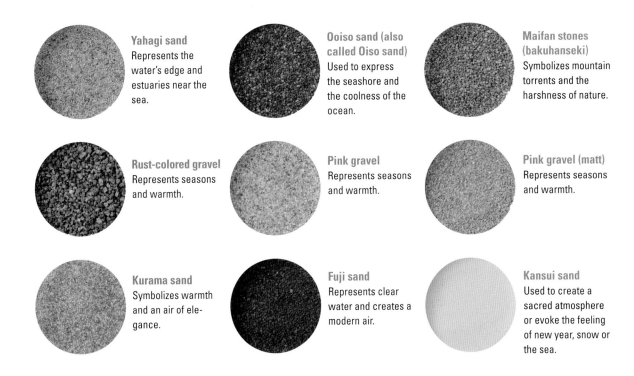

Yahagi sand
Represents the water's edge and estuaries near the sea.

Ooiso sand (also called Oiso sand)
Used to express the seashore and the coolness of the ocean.

Maifan stones (bakuhanseki)
Symbolizes mountain torrents and the harshness of nature.

Rust-colored gravel
Represents seasons and warmth.

Pink gravel
Represents seasons and warmth.

Pink gravel (matt)
Represents seasons and warmth.

Kurama sand
Symbolizes warmth and an air of elegance.

Fuji sand
Represents clear water and creates a modern air.

Kansui sand
Used to create a sacred atmosphere or evoke the feeling of new year, snow or the sea.

Stones

Stones are used in bonsai landscapes, either placed inside pots or used as planters. They express profundity and strength and serve to set off plants' softness. Further, they can determine the direction of the landscape and depending on how they are positioned, can create a sense of perspective. There are various types of rocks, with round ones representing the sea and estuaries while coarse, rough rocks symbolize mountains and mountain torrents. Even a single rock can create various expressions depending on the angle at which it's viewed, the angle at which it's positioned and where it's used in the composition. And, of course, no two rocks look the same. Look for a rock with an interesting appearance and view it from various angles to decide on how to use it.

Ibigawa stones
These stones taken from the Ibi River (Ibi-gawa) which flows through Gifu and Mie prefectures are a mixture of granite and limestone.

Kuroboku stones
Lava from Mt Fuji, sometimes also called bokuseki. They are characterized by their rough surface.

How to Make Basic Potting Soil

Making Potting Soil

The soil used for bonsai landscapes is a combination of those introduced on the previous pages. The most commonly used is a mix of three parts Akadama soil to one part clay soil and one part Fuji sand. This compost is suitable for growing a wide range of plants including pine trees and more. In this book, all the works use this compost, apart from kokedama and azaleas, which like acidic soil. Here, we show you how to blend it.

1. Place three parts soil, one part clay soil and one part Fuji sand in a tub along with slow release fertilizer (base fertilizer).

2. Firstly, mix the Fuji sand and the clay soil together well.

3. Massage the mix of soil, pressing in carefully but firmly until no lumps remain.

4. Gently work the Akadama soil in, as if coating the mix of clay soil and Fuji sand. Take care not to crush the Akadama soil.

5. Once the soil is completely mixed and air has been worked in to make it light and fluffy, it's ready for use.

Compost

Creating a Clay Ball

When making kokedama, use a clay mixture composed of three parts clay soil, one part Akadama soil and one part Fuji sand. These balls of clay soil are of course used to make kokedama, but as they are sticky they can also be used for affixing stones within bonsai settings and attaching moss to vertical surfaces. Mix some so that it's conveniently to hand when you want to use it. To store it, roll it into a ball and place it in a Tupperware container somewhere cool, making sure it doesn't dry out. This way you can use it whenever you like.

1. Add slow release fertilizer (Magamp K) to three parts clay soil, one part Akadama soil and one part Fuji sand and mix together.

2. Mix well, making sure not to crush the Akadama soil.

3. Once the soil is mixed, use a spray bottle to spray a little water at a time onto the soil until it's about as soft as an ear lobe.

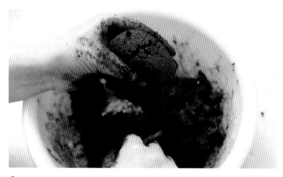

4. If cracks appear, the mixture is not sufficiently blended, so work the soil firmly as if kneading clay until it's thoroughly mixed and becomes sticky.

5. Once the mixture is sticky and glossy, it's ready.

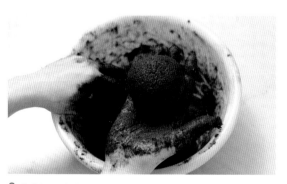

6. Roll into a ball, wrap in plastic wrap and place in a Tupperware container to store.

Making a Bonsai with Multiple Plants

Collective planting bonsai feature multiple plants within the same pot. In general, they are composed from an uneven number of plants of different heights. Additionally, it's important to use plants that have the same growth requirements such as soil acidity or alkalinity. Here, we show you in easy-to-understand steps how to create a group planting using two beech trees and *Coptis quinquefolia*.

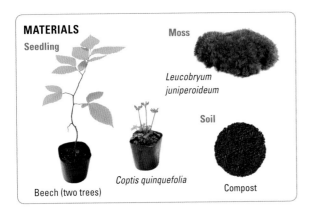

MATERIALS

Seedling

Moss

Leucobryum juniperoideum

Soil

Coptis quinquefolia

Beech (two trees)

Compost

METHOD

1. Use a scoop to cover the base of the pot with stones.

2. Use the scoop to add compost until the base stones are concealed.

3. Remove the beech trees from their pots and use a chopstick to lightly brush off old soil.

4. Trim off excess branches with scissors and neaten each tree's form.

5. Remove the *Coptis quinquefolia* seedling from its pot and spread out the roots. Consider the overall balance of the composition when positioning the seedling and the two beech trees. In this instance, the *Coptis quinquefolia* is visualized as peeking out from the base of the trees, so is planted between the two beeches.

6. Decide on where to position the plants and hold them while pouring soil in so that they sit at the right height for the pot.

7. Once the soil has been added, use your hands to fine tune the position of the plants and adjust the balance of the composition.

8. When the adjustments have been made, poke the chopstick into the soil to guide soil in among the roots. Make sure there is plenty of soil in the back of the arrangement too.

9. Once the soil is compact, add some more. Steady the base of the saplings so they stay put, then use the spatula to flatten the ground to ready it for attaching the moss.

10. Mist water all over the soil to compact it further, watering the plants at the same time.

11. Remove old growth from the underside of the moss you will be planting, forming the right thickness for attaching to the arrangement.

12. Spread moss around the base of the saplings. Use a chopstick to anchor the edge of the moss and press it into the soil.

14. Strew a bit more sand than necessary over the soil surface, then mist water over the arrangement. Then, with your spatula flatten soil to a few millimeters below the edge of the pot.

13. Keep the overall balance in mind while planting the moss. Use a chopstick to poke any moss protruding from the sides of the pot back into the soil.

15. Mist plenty of water over the plants to settle them in and complete the piece.

Making a Kokedama (Moss Ball)

Moss balls are enchanting to look at. They don't require pots, so can be paired with chic platters and interesting containers. There are various methods for creating kokedama. Here, we introduce the technique of using clay soil as the main component for a clay ball, with Akadama soil and Fuji sand added. An *Astilbe japonica* is planted in the ball with moss added and secured with string.

MATERIALS

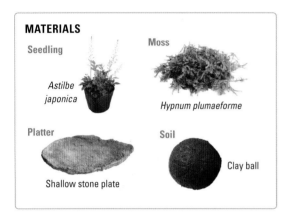

Seedling

Astilbe japonica

Moss

Hypnum plumaeforme

Platter

Shallow stone plate

Soil

Clay ball

METHOD

1. Carefully remove the seedling from the plastic pot, keeping the soil with it so as not to damage the plant.

2. Fill a tub with water and place the plant in it to gently remove soil from the roots with your fingers.

3. In general, remove as much soil as possible, but for plants with flower buds or large leaves, make sure some soil remains.

4. Wrap the roots in a towel to remove excess water.

5. Take some soil from the clay ball and wrap it around the roots, making sure it gets into the gaps between the roots.

6. Keep adding soil a little at a time until the ball is slightly smaller than the intended size, forming it into a round shape.

7. Spread out an adequate amount of moistened *Hypnum plumaeforme* on a dish towel with the foliage facing down.

8. Remove old sections of moss until the sheet of moss is a uniform thickness, then place the seedling on top.

9. Using the dish towel, bring the moss up to cover the ball.

10. Once the whole ball is covered, pat it gently so the moss is lightly wrapped around it.

11. Remove the towel and start winding string around the kokedama in a color that blends in.

12. Wind the string in all directions to secure the moss, making sure not to distort the shape but winding quite firmly.

13. Wind the string around the ball several times to form a uniformly fine mesh pattern in the moss.

14. When the kokedama feels firm and compact, cut the string and roll it into a ball at the end.

15. Use tweezers to push the rounded end of the string into the moss to complete the kokedama.

Making Bonsai with Rock Plantings

Bonsai landscape rock plantings are a bonsai technique that involves planting trees on rocks to create the scenery of craggy mountains, islands in the sea and so on. As the roots entwine with the rock, the richly creative figure of the tree and rock as one entity gives out a sense of the power of nature. Here, we show you how to make a bonsai landscape rock planting using *Carpinus laxiflora* planted in clay soil and wedged between volcanic rocks.

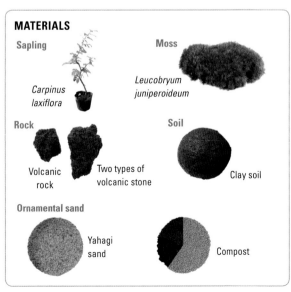

MATERIALS

Sapling

Carpinus laxiflora

Moss

Leucobryum juniperoideum

Rock

Volcanic rock

Two types of volcanic stone

Soil

Clay soil

Ornamental sand

Yahagi sand

Compost

METHOD

1. Use aluminum wire to secure net to the base of the pot and line the pot with stones.

2. Pour in enough soil to cover the stones at the base of the pot.

3. To create a sense of balance, set your rocks with uneven sides facing out and plant the tree between the smooth sides.

4. Remove the sapling from the pot and brush off old soil to free the roots. Cover with soil to conceal the roots.

5. Firstly, attach the clay ball with the sapling planted in it to one of the rocks and press the other rock against it so the ball is wedged between the two rocks.

6. Add more soil, smoothing it out with your fingers so the gap between rock and soil becomes undistinguishable.

7. Lightly cover the base of the pot with soil and place the rocks and sapling on it.

8. Visualize the finished result, including the pot, and adjust the position, overall balance and height.

9. Add more clay soil at the base of the rocks and spread it out to hold the rocks firmly in place. Be careful not to add too much soil, as it will make it hard for the water to drain off.

10. Use a scoop to pour compost into empty spaces in the pot.

11. Use a spatula to flatten the soil, leaving space for the moss and ornamental soil.

12. Spray arrangement liberally with water and press soil with the spatula to firm it.

14. Once the arrangement is in position, trim off excess leaves and neaten the shape of the tree. Pruning redirects strength from the leaves into the roots, so enables roots to form more easily.

13. If moss won't adhere to the clay soil, this is the stage at which to use a spatula to create irregularities in the surface similar to a crag.

15. Attach *Leucobryum juniperoideum* around the base of the rocks. Work from bottom to top as this makes it easier to keep the moss in place.

16. Attach moss firmly to the soil also, using a chopstick to push it into the soil and pressing it lightly with your fingers.

17. Work in the same way to attach moss at the summit of the rocks, pushing in firmly with a chopstick to create undulations.

18. Add moss in at the back of the pot too, pushing in with a chopstick to create undulations and form the landscape.

19. As with the front, work moss along the back, from base to top, pressing firmly.

20. For a natural effect, press moss into crevices along the sides.

21. By adding moss to the base and filling in some gaps in the rock, you achieve a balance of green and earth.

22. Taking care not to cover the edges of the moss, add sand on top of the soil all around, spreading evenly. The effect is one of an island surrounded by sea.

23. Keep a depth of several millimeters between the sand and the edge of the pot. Flatten the sand lightly with the spatula to distribute it well.

24. Use the atomizer liberally to water the soil, settle the plants and rinse the the rock, to complete the landscape.

Watering

Apart from delivering water to plants, watering also plays the role of delivering oxygen needed for respiration to the roots. Basically, give plants plenty of water when the soil dries out. It is fine to water every day, but if the soil is constantly damp it will hinder development. Check the condition of the plants to see whether or not they are absorbing water well and adjust watering accordingly. As a guide to watering throughout the year, give plants plenty of water so they don't dry out during their growth period of spring and summer, and watch out for dehydration and north winds in their dormant period during winter, when they take up less water. Pay particular attention to watering during the height of summer, when it's best to water in the cooler times of the day: morning and evening to night. If plants are extremely dehydrated during the day in midsummer, give them some water, but sometimes water can heat up inside a hose so run it until cold water comes out before watering plants.

 POINT 1 Give plants plenty of water if the soil is dry.

 POINT 2 In summer, water in the morning or evening when it's cooler.

POINT 3 Take care plants don't dry out during winter.

Watering Outdoors

If you think the soil has dried out, direct plenty of water into the soil in the pot, at the same time checking that it's draining properly. Use either a hose or watering can.

Keep watering until water drains out from the hole in the pot. Poor drainage causes root decay, so check that water is draining properly.

Watering Indoors

For surfaces covered in moss

Hold the pot in the sink and gently spray water over the moss. Lightly knead the surface with your hands to work the water in.

For surfaces covered in ornamental sand

If pots covered in ornamental sand are watered in the usual way, the sand will spill out, so either use a watering can or cup water in your hand to gently pour a large amount over the arrangement.

When watering is not possible and soil has completely dried out

If you're going to be away from home for a few days or if the soil has dried out and isn't taking in water, place the pot in a tub full of water and allow it to be absorbed through the base.

For kokedama

Fill a tub with water and place the kokedama in it, gently kneading it in the water. Moss turns a whitish color when it's dry. Kokedama are particularly prone to drying out so make sure to check them regularly.

Preventing Disease

Disease is the archenemy of bonsai. Diseased trees lose their form and in particularly bad cases can wither and die, so it's vital to take precautionary measures. Boost plants' resilience through daily care so that they grow strong and resistant to pests. Carefully select horticultural preparations. Regular applications of fungicide in the concentration recommended by the manufacturer provide constant protection against pests. When applying chemicals, choose a day that is still and cloudy. Wear a mask and rubber gloves to prevent inhaling or ingesting any of the chemicals, and work outside. Regardless of how much care you take in growing bonsai, it's impossible to completely prevent damage to the plant. If it starts showing worrying symptoms, early response and appropriate action are key. The diseases that particularly affect bonsai are powdery mildew, leaf blight, black point and brown spot. First of all, remove any affected leaves and branches and apply specific treatments. Affected leaves can spread the condition if they fall, so incineration is recommended. Isolate the plant. If it still does not recover after several applications of treatment, consult staff at a bonsai specialty store or nursery. Disinfect your tools after treating a diseased plant.

Powdery mildew
Leaves appear to be completely covered in white powder. Occurs easily in periods of low humidity and may kill the plant. A disinfectant called Trifmine is effective against it.

Leaf blight
Small brown blotches appear on leaves. Occurs easily in periods of high humidity, so keep out of the rain during prolonged rainy periods. Remove and destroy affected leaves and branches and apply chemical treatment to the plant.

Black point
Black blotches like sunspots appear on leaves. These expand out, the affected area turns yellow and leaves fall off. Occurs frequently during rainy seasons and other times when humidity is high. Remove and destroy affected leaves and apply chemical treatment to the plant.

Brown spot
This disease is caused by a threadlike bacterium that spreads, causing leaves to wither and drop. When many leaves are diseased the tree's growth is adversely affected. Remove dead leaves and apply appropriate treatment to the plant.

Chemical Treatments Effective Against Disease

Topjin
Disinfectant in a paste form that is applied to cuts left after pruning or to areas where parts of the tree have been removed due to disease. Allows the wound to heal faster and prevents disease-causing bacteria from infecting the tree.

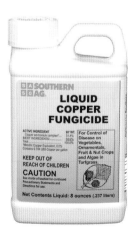

Southern AG Liquid Copper Fungicide
This is available in liquid and powder formulas, and there are a number of brands available. Bear in mind that different fungi can require different types of fungicide.

Pest Control

Different tree types attract different pests, but the most common pests that affect bonsai are aphids, scale insects, spider mites and slugs. They may be concealed on the undersides of leaves or under pots. Check plants regularly and destroy pests as soon as you find them.

Aphids
These mature quickly and multiply rapidly, clustering around new shoots and leaf stems. In addition to weakening leaves by feeding on sap, they can transmit diseases to your plants. Check plants often and treat with the insecticide of your choice when needed.

Scale insects
This parasite infests leaves, stems and branches, feeding on sap. Their excrement can cause sooty mold. Apply lime sulfur in trees' dormant season as a preventive measure, but if there is an infestation, use a toothbrush to brush them off or treat with the insecticide of your choice.

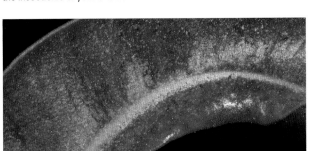

Spider mites
This parasite infests the underside of leaves, feeding on their sap. This results in telltale white splash-like patterns on the leaves. Infestations occur in hot weather with low humidity.

Slugs
Slugs damage new buds and flowers by feeding on them at night. They are more numerous during rainy seasons. Catch and kill them or exterminate them with a solution specifically for slugs. Left in a container near bonsai pots, beer will attract them and they will then drown in it.

Chemical Treatments Effective Against Pests

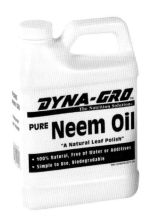

Dyna-Gro Pure Neem Oil
Available under numerous brand names, neem oil is an organic miticide, insecticide and fungicide that can be safely used on most plants.

Safer Insect Killing Soap
Insecticidal detergents can be a less toxic chemical means of eliminating pests. These come in concentrated and ready-to-use formulas. Some growers advocate a solution of dishwashing liquid and water .

Fertilizer

As bonsai are grown in the limited space inside pots, they can suffer from a lack of nutrients. It is necessary to feed them with a fertilizer containing a balanced mixture of nitrogen, phosphate and potassium, making sure to use the amount recommended in the accompanying instructions and apply it at the appropriate time. Here, we introduce some of the types of fertilizer to use on bonsai landscapes.

EarthPods Bamboo + Bonsai Organic Plant Food Spikes

A slow-release formula that feeds bonsai over a period of 2–3 weeks. Capsules can be pushed into soil, or opened and the contents spread around the roots. They deliver nutrients, trace minerals, beneficial fungi and hormones.

Dyna-Gro Bonsai-Pro Liquid Plant Food 7-9-5

Liquids can offer a complete diet of essential nutrients. Dilute as directed to ensure healthy ratios.

Superfly Bonsai Professional Bonsai Fertilizer

Smaller pellets can deliver nutrients quickly and effectively, and can continue delivering for several weeks.

HB-101 Liquid Bonsai Plant Vitalizer

Various Japanese fertilizers are available through online vendors and fine nurseries. They provide optimal nutrition for a variety of plant types when diluted to suit specific plants' requirements.

**Biogold Original
Natural organic fertilizer**

A solid type of fertilizer that is placed on top of the soil. It is an organic fertilizer that is processed at high temperatures and is odorless when watered. For a pot 6 in (15 cm) in diameter, sprinkle about 15 pellets on to the soil.

Micrototal

Foliar sprays are another nutrient delivery system. These can be used directly on foliage or as a soil drench during watering.

A Maintenance Calendar

JANUARY

It's time to repot plants that have grown too big for their pots or whose pots have cracked due to cold. On cold days, move pots under cover or indoors so their roots are not damaged.

FEBRUARY

Pots may crack due to cold, so move them indoors. Once the cold is less harsh, cut grasses at the roots to remove withered growth and allow new sprouts to emerge. It's also the time to prune plum trees. Once the flowers finish blooming, cut branches two to three nodes from the base.

MARCH

This is the time of year when plants start regenerating. Steadily increase the frequency of watering and bring the plant inside as strong spring winds can damage new growth. Once cherry blossom season is over, cherry trees take in a lot of water, so observe their condition and alter watering accordingly.

APRIL

All plants experience growth during April and May, so make sure fertilizing and watering are properly carried out. Place plants outside in plenty of sun. This time of year is suitable for maintenance such as repotting, dividing stock, group planting and training trees on an angle.

MAY

Plants continue to develop and grow well at this time of year. It's the right time to prune maples. There are a lot of insects around so improve air circulation to prevent disease and pest infestations. Give plants that have finished flowering another round of fertilizer.

JUNE

Humidity levels are high at this time of year and it gets steamy, so keep an eye on growth, watching out for disease and improving air circulation. Cut the leaves off *Zelkova*. If you nip off the buds that emerged in the spring, the leaves that grow in summer will be fine and delicate.

JULY

As the hot weather continues, pay attention to plants drying out and water once in the morning and once in the evening. Place plants in shade and use a liquid fertilizer to prevent the leaves burning. Finish pruning red pines by about the middle of the month.

AUGUST

Pay particular attention to plants drying out at this time of year. If you go on a long holiday, leave your bonsai with a specialist store who will water and maintain them. Finish pruning black pines by the middle of the month.

SEPTEMBER

Beware of the lingering summer heat. Once it starts to fade, divide plant stock, repot and carry out other maintenance. Move plants that were kept in the shade during summer to a place where they can get plenty of sun. Furthermore, give plants plenty of fertilizer at this time in order to stimulate growth the following year.

OCTOBER

Fruiting plants bear fruit at this time of year. Harvest fruit early to lessen the strain on the tree. Make sure plants get plenty of sunlight and fertilize well to improve root growth. It's a good time to prune, train trees using wire, repot and divide plant stock.

NOVEMBER

In the outskirts of cities, leaves begin to change color. Make sure plants are kept somewhere they can feel the difference between day and night temperatures to bring on their fall colors. Remove moss and ornamental sand from plants that grew vigorously over spring and summer to make respiration easier.

DECEMBER

Carry out maintenance on bonsai to use as Christmas or New Year decorations. Evergreens play the leading role at this time of year. If cherry trees are not allowed to feel the cold, they will not blossom, so keep them outdoors from now until March.

Plant Catalog

*A dash in the "pages used" column indicates plants that are not utilized in the landscapes in this book.

● TREES: EVERGREENS WITH NEEDLE FOLIAGE

SPECIES	CHARACTERISTICS AND COMMENTS	FLOWERING SEASON	PAGES USED
Red pine *Pinaceae	A pine with reddish bark on the trunk, it grows naturally in mountainous regions. Also known in Japanese as the "woman pine" due to its elegant branches and leaves. Is resilient to dryness. Give plenty of water when the soil surface dries out.	—	41
Ezo spruce *Pinaceae	Naturally occurring mainly in Hokkaido, this pine grows into a tall tree. It is recognizable by its dense, pale green foliage. Keep in a spot that receives a lot of sun. Designated the official tree of Hokkaido, it's a good choice when wanting to express the natural environment of northern regions.	—	17, 40, 45
Black pine *Pinaceae	Grows naturally along the west coast of Japan's main island. In Japanese it's also known as the "man pine" due to its strong leaves, thick branches and dark colored bark on its trunk. Used for bonsai since olden times, it's displayed in the entrance hall and other prominent spots during the New Year period in Japan.	—	—
Japanese white pine *Pinaceae	Its foliage, which grows in five short needles, lends it the name "five-needle pine." Keep in well drained soil that is on the dry side. It is seen as auspicious to display one of these trees in the entrance hall during the New Year period in Japan.	—	48

● TREES: EVERGREENS

SPECIES	CHARACTERISTICS AND COMMENTS	FLOWERING SEASON	PAGES USED
Evergreen ash *Oleaceae	An evergreen or semi-evergreen tree. Flowers from May to June with many small blossoms on large panicles. Its attractive small glossy leaves and its form, which sways lightly in the breeze, make it an appealing tree which is popular in gardens.	May to June	34
Chinese juniper *Cupressaceae	Grows naturally on the cliffs of high mountains along the coastline. A relative of the pyramid Chinese juniper, it indicates *Juniperus chinensis*. Its dense foliage and the tendency of the trunk to grow in horizontal curves make for a tree that is enjoyable to train into various shapes and forms.	—	13
Tsuyama cypress *Cupressaceae	A variety of cypress discovered in Tsuyama, Okayama prefecture. If it receives too much water it grows spindly, and should be kept outdoors in a place where air circulates well. Nip off growth by hand when pruning. It is a slow grower, so suits a small pot.	—	—
Japanese cypress *Cupressaceae	An evergreen tree. Entwined in Japanese traditions since olden times, it's also used as a building material. It comes in several cultivars and has delicate branches that grow out horizontally to form a dense ovoid shaped tree crown.	—	14, 27, 49

● TREES: DECIDUOUS TREES

SPECIES	CHARACTERISTICS AND COMMENTS	FLOWERING SEASON	PAGES USED
Japanese maple *Aceraceae	Growing on the Japan Sea side north of the Kinki region, this tree is in the same lineage as *Acer palmatum var. matsumurae*. From spring to summer, the green of its weeping branches creates a cooling impression. It has delicate leaves that turn red in the fall. The tree itself is strong and grows vigorously.	—	15
Chinese elm *Ulmaceae	This tree flowers around September and fruits in November, giving it the Japanese name of "fall elm." In the fall its leaves change to splendid yellows and reds, and this beauty has led to this tree's widespread use as a bonsai.	—	10
Virginia creeper *Vitaceae	A vine originally from north America, this plant is a deep purple when it's putting forth buds, turning a dark green afterwards and red in the fall. It should be grown in a sunny spot. Place it somewhere that has different levels to enjoy its leaves trailing down.	—	—
Japanese weeping maple *Aceraceae	From spring to fall, this tree has attractive reddish brown leaves. Its weeping figure is elegant and its delicately divided leaf tips recall the spray from a waterfall. Keep in partial shade.	—	21, 47

SPECIES	CHARACTERISTICS AND COMMENTS	FLOWERING SEASON	PAGES USED
Korean hornbeam *Betulaceae	In nature, this small tree takes root even on cliffs with little soil. Its small leaves and the unique bark on its trunk make it popular. Takes a long time to shed its leaves even after they turn yellow.	—	25
Liquidambar *Aceraceae	This tree is appreciated for its new greenery in May, changing colors in the fall and bare elegance in winter. Its leaves do not turn as deep a red as a Japanese maple in the fall, but its mix of yellow and red lend it a different kind of elegance.	4, 5	—
Carpinus japonica *Betulaceae	A small deciduous tree. In Japan, it's known as *kanashide* when grown as a bonsai but as *kumashide* ("four bear paws") when grown as a regular plant. The fine veins in the leaves create the look of delicate leaves.	—	25
Kinmenirekeyaki (*Zelkova*) *Ulmaceae	A variety of Chinese elm with attractive golden leaves. Keep in a sunny place where air circulates well. There are various types of Chinese elm. This one is known for the refined look of its branches.	—	—
Zelkova *Ulmaceae	A deciduous tree with an attractive form that gives it a trusted position as a bonsai. With its beautiful changing leaves in the fall and flowers in the spring, it brings pleasure year round. It is fast-growing so is enjoyable to cultivate.	—	38
Acer sieboldianum Miq. *Aceraceae	As its leaves are smaller than that of the *Acer japonicum* (Japanese feather fan maple) it resembles, this is the *small* Japanese feather fan maple. It enjoys a sunny spot and from around October to November its leaves change color – not to red, but to an attractive yellow.	May	—
Styrax japonicus "Pendulus" *Styracaceae	A small tree that is a cultivar of the Styracaceae family, it has white flowers from May to June. It has an attractive form which can be enjoyed year round, even after its leaves have dropped. It is tolerant to shade, robust and easy to grow.	May to June	—
Hornbeam *Betulaceae	Earlier to bud than other trees, the hornbeam prompts thoughts that spring is on the way ("soro soro haru"), giving it the name *soro* in Japanese. A stereotypical small tree, it's sometimes used to portray scenery around villages.	April to May	—
Chinese Virginia creeper *Vitaceae	Resistant to cold. Kept in a sunny spot, its leaves will turn beautiful colors. In bonsai landscapes, it's particularly attractive when shaped to resemble a precipice.	—	20
Acer palmatum "Deshojo" *Aceraceae	At the start of fall, the deep yellow-green leaves take on some red tones, turning a deep crimson later into the season. Likes a sunny spot where air circulates well. Keep in partial shade in summer.	—	16
Vaccinium old-hamii *Ericaceae	A low growing deciduous shrub. The changing colors are attractive in summer. Around May to June, numerous flowers bloom, with fruit maturing to a black color around August to October. It likes acidic soils, so add Kanuma pumice to its soil.	May to June	—
Plantae Rosales *Rosaceae	White flowers bloom in late spring and early summer. Leaves are long, slender and jagged-edged . In the fall, the leaves color vividly and the plant produces red berries.	May	—
Premna japonica *Lamiaceae	Also known as *jakou momiji* (maple), its leaves give off an unpleasant odor when rubbed, giving it the nickname of "musk maple." It grows a lot of small branches so is easy to shape.	—	31
Ulmus parvifolia *Ulmaceae (see also Chinese Elm)	A deciduous tree that grows quickly and is easily made into a bonsai. Water liberally when its soil dries out. Its vigorous growth means it requires regular pruning, making it a good tree for beginners who want to learn how to prune.	—	10

● TREES: EVERGREENS WITH NEEDLE FOLIAGE

SPECIES	CHARACTERISTICS AND COMMENTS	FLOWERING SEASON	PAGES USED
Sorbaria kirilowii *Rosaceae	Has small white flowers from June to August and fruits from September to November. Cultivate in a sunny spot.	June to August	—
Acer japonicum *Aceraceae	A deciduous tree in the Aceraceae family.	—	29, 30
Wax tree *Anacardiaceae	The leaves if this small tree, also referred to as the wax tree maple, change to beautiful colors in the fall. Its residue is not as strong as sumac but can cause allergic reactions, so take care when handling.	—	43
Pink wild rose *Rosaceae	One of the modern roses, this cultivar is a complex hybrid that has been bred and refined over many years. As it's a climbing type, it's appreciated for its flowers and branches. In the fall, it has red fruit.	April to August	21
Beech *Fagaceae	A deciduous tree native to Japan which forms forests in the wild. The leaves burn in direct sunlight, so keep in partial shade and make sure it doesn't dry out. Train it with wire after the leaves have dropped and enjoy the wait until spring arrives.	—	32
Mikawa Yatsubusa maple *Aceraceae	A cultivar of *Acer palmatum var. Matsumurae*. It is defined by its short nodes and fine leaves. In spring the tips of the leaves turn red, and they change color in the fall. The gaps between the branches are short and the foliage is dense so it's possible to form into a round shape.	—	—
Maple *Aceraceae	Its new green foliage delights from spring to early summer, with color turning a vibrant red as fall progresses. Likes sunny places with good air flow. Move to a place with shade in summer and keep under cover in winter.	April to May	—
Japanese maple (*Acer palmatum var. Matsumurae*)	There is a sense of Japanese refinement in the attractive fall colors of this tree. Keep out of direct sunlight and bring indoors in the height of summer. Trimmed, maintained trees are generally available to purchase from May to June and are recommended for beginners.	April to May	37

● TREES: SEMI-DECIDUOUS TREES

SPECIES	CHARACTERISTICS AND COMMENTS	FLOWERING SEASON	PAGES USED
Serissa japonica *Rubiaceae	Has small white or lilac flowers in spring and fall. As it's an evergreen, its greenery can be enjoyed even in winter. Keep in a sunny spot where air circulates well, but move indoors or into a protected area in winter.	May to July	9, 44
Chinese fringe flower *Hamamelidaceae	A small evergreen tree. It blossoms around May, with flowers made up of four long, slender green-tinged cream petals that form clusters. The tree occasionally has a few flowers in the fall too	April to May	33
Ash *Oleaceae	Distinguished by its small glossy leaves, this plant should be kept in a sunny spot year round. It likes humid places and does not endure extreme heat, so care needs to be taken in summer.	May to June	12
Cotoneaster *Rosaceae	A plant in the rosaceae family, originating in China. The branches slant out horizontally. From about May to June, it has pink flowers and in the fall red fruits about ¼ in (5 mm)-sized fruit on its branches. If its branches are cut back while it's dormant, it will blossom well.	May to June	—

● GRASSES: EVERGREEN

SPECIES	CHARACTERISTICS AND COMMENTS	FLOWERING SEASON	PAGES USED
Woodsia polystichoides Eaton *Woodsiaceae	A medium sized fern which grows on rocks in rocky areas. Likes sun, so keep in sun or partial shade and water well. If grown in a pot it forms a small but defined specimen plant.	—	19
Sasa glabra "Minor" *Gramineae	The general name for the dwarf variety of *Sasa veitchii* of which there are more than 10 different types. To achieve a uniform height, trim or thin out the plants. However, trimming in summer can cause the leaves to wither, so it's best to do it in spring.	—	22
Ophiopogon japonicus Ker.f.nanus fort *Convallariaceae	A relative of *Ophiogon japonicus* which is resilient against cold and heat, this plant is used as ground cover as well as in gardens and in bonsai arrangements.	—	73
Ophiopogon japonicus Ker.f.nanus fort *Convallariaceae	A relative of *Ophiogon japonicus* which is resilient against cold and heat, this plant is used as ground cover as well as in gardens and in bonsai arrangements.	—	73
Asplenium trichomanes *Aspleniaceae	The Japanese name of "tea whisk fern" comes from the plant's resemblance to the implement used in the tea ceremony. Its delicate leaves and attractive form lead it to be used as a fern that adds elegance at ground level in bonsai landscapes.	—	19
Horsetail *Equisetum prealtum* *Equisetaceae	A fern that inhabits swampy areas, it is robust and withstands dryness well, allowing it to be grown in or out of doors. It is often used to resemble bamboo in bonsai so is used as New Year bonsai and for other arrangements that evoke bamboo.	—	36
Hakuryu *Convallariaceae	A hardy evergreen perennial that has foliage year round. Can be used in group plantings as the perfect accompaniment to the main tree and is useful for adjusting the volume of greenery in an arrangement. Also recommended for western style group plantings.	—	—
Tofieldia nuda *Acoraceae	A small perennial plant that grows in damp rocky areas. It has a pretty white flower that grows on a stem from between the leaves.	April to June	24
Angiopteris lygodiifolia *Marattiaceae	A large evergreen fern native to tropical and subtropical rainforests. In Japan it's native to the south coast of the main island and south of the Izu peninsula and is often used as an ornamental foliage plant.	—	11
Arundinariinae *Gramineae	A cultivar of *Pleioblastus pygmaeus var.distichus*, this plant is short with dense foliage. It is used as undergrowth and can be used in scenery that recalls a grassy plain.	—	32

● GRASSES: DECIDUOUS

SPECIES	CHARACTERISTICS AND COMMENTS	FLOWERING SEASON	PAGES USED
Hakonechloa macra *Gramineae	A perennial that grows in mountain regions, the cliffs of canyons and similar terrains. It flutters attractively in the wind and is popular among bonsai aficionados. It likes partial shade and moderate humidity but does not cope with dryness, so take care to water as needed.	July to September	15, 23
Miscanthus sinensis f. gracillimus *Gramineae	A perennial that withstands cold well, this is a cultivar of the pampas grass native to the Japanese countryside. The leaves are as fine as threads, giving it a different kind of elegance to that of pampas grass.	August to October	42
Aster scaber *Asteraceae	Grows in forests in plains and hill areas, dry areas and by the side of the road. Has many small white flowers in the fall.	September to November	28

● GRASSES: DECIDUOUS

SPECIES	CHARACTERISTICS AND COMMENTS	FLOWERING SEASON	PAGES USED
Aruncus aethusifolius *Saxifragaceae	A perennial originating on the Korean peninsula. The "tanna" part of its Japanese name, *tanna chidakesashi*, refers to the ancient name for what is now Jeju Island. Grows between 4-8 in (10–20 cm) tall and suits group plantings. The stems tinged red like coral are a defining feature.	May to July	28
Bouteloua gracilis *Gramineae	The flower spikes grow out horizontally and resemble a fish called *medaka*, giving this mountain grass its Japanese name of *medaka sou* ("medaka grass"). Suits group plantings. Dislikes humidity but is vulnerable when dried out, so place in a spot with good air circulation and make sure it receives plenty of water.	June to July	24

● GRASSES: SEMI- DECIDUOUS

SPECIES	CHARACTERISTICS AND COMMENTS	FLOWERING SEASON	PAGES USED
Selaginella moellendorffii *Selaginellaceae	Grows in clusters on rocks and trees in forests of warm regions. Most of its branches grow out in a radial fashion, giving the plant the overall look of a tree. When dry, the branches wither and curl inwards but will spread out again once they receive moisture.	—	19, 31, 33

● FRUITING PLANTS

SPECIES	CHARACTERISTICS AND COMMENTS	FLOWERING SEASON	PAGES USED
Akebi *Lardizabalaceae	The split fruit of this plant resembles a wide open mouth, and it's said that its name derives from this (ake-bi = open fruit). The small, oval shaped leaves grow in palmate form in groups of five. It is a monoecious plant with diclinous flowers. If cultivating in a small pot, it should be repotted every year.	April to May	—
Japanese andromeda *Ericaceae	An evergreen that is used in Japanese gardens and landscaped gardens. It is toxic and takes its Japanese name of "drunken horse tree" from horses eating the leaves and appearing intoxicated. It has white flowers, but those of this cultivar are pink.	February to April	—
Ardisia crispa *Myrsinaceae	Comparable with the "10000-ryo" (*manryo*) this plant known as the "100-ryo" (*hyakuryo*) was highly valued in the Edo period and was famous for not being purchasable for less than 100 ryo (a now obsolete unit of currency). It has larger leaves and fruit than the manryo and the leaves are a darker color. It is best viewed from November to March, when it fruits.	July	—
Diplomorpha sikokiana *Thymelaeaceae	A robust plant that is easy to cultivate, it has become popular in recent years. Its fibers are used as raw material for paper. It has no petals but puts forth flower heads in early summer and fruits in winter, so can be enjoyed for both its flowers and fruit.	October to December	—
Cherry *Rosaceae	Has white flowers in clusters of two to four and fruits from May to June once it has finished blossoming. Likes cool climates, so place in partial shade in midsummer. Does not withstand rain well so place in a sunny spot with good air circulation.	April	—
Ardisia crenata *Myrsinaceae	A small evergreen shrub with attractive fruit, which can be white or yellow depending on the cultivar. Fertilize well to ensure bountiful fruit. It is best viewed from November to January when it fruits.	July	—
Ardisia japonica *Myrsinaceae	Also known as *juryo* ("10-ryo"), this is a garden plant from olden times beloved of the citizens of Edo. While its fruit is bountiful and it is auspicious around new year, its Christmassy appearance means it can represent that season also. It is best viewed from November to February when it fruits.	July to August	—

● FLOWERING PLANTS

SPECIES	CHARACTERISTICS AND COMMENTS	FLOWERING SEASON	PAGES USED
Asahiyama sakura *Rosaceae	The cold of winter activates blossoms on this plant. Once it has flower buds, bring it indoors. After blossoming it takes in a lot of water so make sure to water properly. Prune branches after the leaves have dropped off.	March to April	—
Soldanella alpine *Primulaceae	Japanese name, which equates to "false fringed galax," comes from its resemblance to that plant. The roots have a refreshing scent. Looks cute when used as ground cover in scenery that incorporates rocks, such as the sides of rivers.	May to August	19
Leptospermum scoparium *Myrtaceae	An evergreen shrub originating in New Zealand, the beauty of its vivid red flowers has made it popular in places such as north America and Taiwan. The color and shape of the flowers lead it to often be used to represent peach or plum trees in bonsai landscapes.	November to May	—
Saotome azalea *Ericaceae	A cultivar of Rhododendron obtusa that does not readily flower. It is enjoyed for its leaves, which are characteristically fine. Prune from summer to fall. Scars form if the leaves are cut, so cut from the branches, working to create a rounded shape.	October to November	—
Saxifraga polyanglica *Saxifragaceae	An alpine plant with lots of small flowers. Moist, hot conditions do not suit it so place it in a spot where air circulates well and water less frequently in summer. There are many varieties, so it's fun finding one whose flowers appeal.	February to April	—
Cornus officinalis *Cornaceae	This deciduous shrub in the Cornaceae family is well known for its flowers, which are used tea ceremonies. As its yellow flowers blossom in about March, earlier than cherry blossoms, they are the first to signal the approach of spring. In late fall, it has red fruit to enjoy.	March	—
Rhodotypos *Rosaceae	Has white flowers in spring. The leaves are a vibrant green and the branches hang down slightly. It is often used as a garden tree so is a good option when wanting to create a gardening scene.	April to May	—
Camellia *Theaceae	Has large flowers from winter to spring and attractively glossy leaves that make it impressive even at the small size of a bonsai. There are some sturdy varieties, which are easy to grow, and many cultivars. Caterpillars are attracted to these plants so take necessary precautions.	February to April	—
Coptis quinquefolia *Ranunculaceae	A perennial in the Ranunculaceae family. It blossoms at the start of spring with flowers that resemble plum blossoms, giving it a name in Japanese that equates to "plum flower coptis." It is an evergreen and has white flowers when few other plants are blossoming, lending it to use in group plantings.	March to May	—
Houstonia *Rubiaceae	A mountain grass originating in north America. Its small flowers have given it the name *hinakusa* ("doll grass") in Japanese. Works well planted at the base of trees to provide flowers. Keep in a place with good air flow and beware of humidity.	March to June	—
Anemone hortensis *Ranunculaceae	Distinguished by its pink flowers, in summer it sports only foliage. It is one of the grasses more susceptible to humidity, so place in a spot where air circulates well. Recommended as a plant to go with a cherry tree in a group planting.	April to May	—
Ranunculus ficaria (purple) *Ranunculaceae	This Ranunculus ficaria is a type that has dark purple leaves. It works well in group plantings to set off other flowers. This type requires fertilizing and a spot where air circulates well.	April	—
Solanum japonense Nakai *Solanaceae	A climbing evergreen perennial in the Solanaceae family, it has purple to white flowers in April to July. Resilient against pests and easy to cultivate, but if using in a group planting, make sure it doesn't grow so much that it puts pressure on other plants.	April to July	—
Caltha palustris var. nipponica *Ranunculaceae	An alpine plant that grows over winter and blossoms at the start of spring. It is dormant over summer so water to keep soil moist during this period. This type requires fertilizing and a spot where air circulates well.	February to June	—
Forsythia *Oleaceae	A deciduous shrub. It is used in gardens and along city thoroughfares and has dense yellow flowers in early spring. Its roots have a tendency to coil, so repot regularly. With its attractive leaves in summer and changing colors in the fall, this shrub can be enjoyed year round.	March to April	22

SPECIES	CHARACTERISTICS AND COMMENTS	FLOWERING SEASON	PAGES USED
Leucobryum bowringii Mitt. *Leucobryum	Also known by other names such as mountain moss. When damp, it becomes a deeper green, turning white when dried out. From April to October, keep in partial shade, and keep in a dark place over summer.	—	51, 52
Bryum argenteum *Bryaceae	A compact moss that grows in clumps on soil, stone walls and so on in sunny places. Copes well with dryness and turns a silvery color when it absorbs water. Enjoys direct sunlight but make sure it doesn't steam up.	—	—
Racomitrium japonicum *Racomitriumceae	Grows in yellow-green clusters in rocky areas that get plenty of sun, such as river beds and mountain regions. Copes well with direct sunlight and cold so is easy to look after. It has short irregular branches and can be used as undergrowth.	—	16
Hypnum plumaeforme	Best suited to partially shaded, slightly humid areas. It is possible to grow it in sunny places but it may take on a yellowish tinge. It can be found where Racomitrium japonicum grows, so they can be planted together.	—	—
Leucobryum juniperoideum *Dicranaceae	Forms rounded mounds that are nice to touch. If kept fairly dry in a spot that receives good sunlight it will grow like white hair. It can be cultivated in sunny places but in direct sunlight the leaves burn and go brown.	—	12, 17, 19–25, 27, 29, 33–8, 40–1, 43–5, 47–51

Published by Tuttle Publishing, an imprint of Periplus Editions (HK) Ltd.

www.tuttlepublishing.com

Hajimete no Keshiki Bonsai: Keshiki wo Hachi no Naka de Hyougensuru Hassou to Kotsu
Copyright © 2013 by Kenji Kobayashi
English translation rights arranged with Seibundo Shinkosha
Publishing Co. Ltd. through Japan UNI Agency, Inc., Tokyo

Translation copyright © 2018 by Periplus Editions(HK) Ltd.
Translated from Japanese by Leeyong Soo

ISBN 978-4-8053-1482-1

Library of Congress Number 2018943063

STAFF
Photography: Natsu Tanimoto, Naomi Muto, Chihiro Tanaka
Cover Design: Mano Design Office
Developmental editing: Misaki Kiya
Editorial services: DTP Flare
Illustrations: Tomomi Itabashi

Distributed by
North America, Latin America & Europe
Tuttle Publishing
364 Innovation Drive, North Clarendon, VT 05759-9436 U.S.A.
Tel: 1 (802) 773-8930; Fax: 1 (802) 773-6993
info@tuttlepublishing.com; www.tuttlepublishing.com

Japan
Tuttle Publishing
Yaekari Building, 3rd Floor, 5-4-12 Osaki, Shinagawa-ku, Tokyo 141 0032
Tel: (81) 3 5437-0171, Fax: (81) 3 5437-0755
sales@tuttle.co.jp; www.tuttle.co.jp

Asia Pacific
Berkeley Books Pte. Ltd.
61 Tai Seng Avenue #02-12, Singapore 534167
Tel: (65) 6280-1330; Fax: (65) 6280-6290
inquiries@periplus.com.sg; www.periplus.com

Printed in China   1807RR
21 20 19 18   10 9 8 7 6 5 4 3 2 1

About Tuttle "Books to Span the East and West"

Our core mission at Tuttle Publishing is to create books which bring people together one page at a time. Tuttle was founded in 1832 in the small New England town of Rutland, Vermont (USA). Our fundamental values remain as strong today as they were then—to publish best-in-class books informing the English-speaking world about the countries and peoples of Asia. The world has become a smaller place today and Asia's economic, cultural and political influence has expanded, yet the need for meaningful dialogue and information about this diverse region has never been greater. Since 1948, Tuttle has been a leader in publishing books on the cultures, arts, cuisines, languages and literatures of Asia. Our authors and photographers have won numerous awards and Tuttle has published thousands of books on subjects ranging from martial arts to paper crafts. We welcome you to explore the wealth of information available on Asia at **www.tuttlepublishing.com**.